WHAT MEN DON'T TELL WOMEN ABOUT BUSINESS

OPENING UP THE HEAVILY GUARDED ALPHA MALE PLAYBOOK

Christopher V. Flett

BICENTENNIAL

1807

WILEY

2007

BICENTENNIAL

JOHN WILEY & SONS, INC.

Published by John Wiley & Sons, Inc., Hoboken, New Jersey.
Published simultaneously in Canada.

Wiley Bicentennial Logo: Richard J. Pacifico.

For general information on our other products and services please contact our Customer Care Department within the United States at (800) 762-2974, outside the United States at (317) 572-3993 or fax (317) 572-4002.

Wiley also publishes its books in a variety of electronic formats. Some content that appears in print may not be available in electronic books. For more information about Wiley products, visit our web site at www.wiley.com.

Library of Congress Cataloging-in-Publication Data

Flett, Christopher V., 1974–
    What men don't tell women about business: opening up the heavily guarded alpha male playbook/Christopher V. Flett.
        p. cm.
    "Published simultaneously in Canada."
    ISBN 978-0-470-14508-1 (cloth)
  1. Women—Employment. 2. Sex role in the work environment.
  3. Sexual division of labor. 4. Men—Psychology. 5. Success in business.
  6. Communication in organizations—Sex differences. I. Title.
    HD6053.F555 2008
    650.1082—dc22

                                                        2007015886

Printed in the United States of America.

10 9 8 7 6 5 4 3 2 1

Contents

Preface

If you look at the business books coming out today, you'll see men offering hunting stories of how they built their companies. They talk about the glory of success and being No. 1 among all their peers. Men read these success stories and aspire to be the same, to do the same. We want to fight to the top, take a moment to enjoy the view, and then look for the next mountain to climb. Men have a difficult time focusing on the process. It is all about the goal for us, not the process. We aren't interested in how he did it. We want to know the feeling of success, and we'll figure out how we'll get there later.

Women, on the other hand, write books on how women can understand men in business and how to swim with those sharks. Female authors that I have read spend a lot of time giving women advice on how to move ahead in business by staying clear of the Alpha Male. These female authors present this avoidance tactic as their process for being successful. However, when you avoid working relationships with successful and driven individuals any success that could have been realized is missed as well.

These authors suggest this program of avoidance based on their past experiences and their interpretations of these experiences. It is an understandable perspective, especially a generation ago when women were just finding out what kind of space they could occupy in the workforce. Yet these authors and their perspectives are disadvantaged precisely because they're women and don't know what men are really thinking. And that's where I come in. While my perspective is also born from personal experience, I must admit that I am one of the men you would be told to avoid. Alpha Males absolutely put the glass ceiling in place, but it has been the professional woman who has held it there. By breaking the patterns of giving up one's power and stopping the attack of other women, a female professional can not only gain equality in the workplace, but also step into a leadership position left vacant by an Alpha Male in the old paradigm of business. The greatest enemy to women in business is women in business—specifically those who consciously attack one another trying to get on the guy's team and those who willingly continue to give up their power to men and act as role models for other women to do the same.

This book is not a glory story. It is not a 21st century version of a fairytale where the damsel in distress becomes the entrepreneurial CEO. This book is a true account of how a man sees business and women in business. This is not meant to be a critique nor a list of suggestions of how women need to change. Instead I want to share with female readers how men think and behave in the business setting and how they interpret the behavior of women.

This isn't a war, rather it's a long overdue conversation. I make no apologies for the pages that follow. This is meant to be the start of a conversation and not the beginning and end of a conversation. I take responsibility for starting the fire, but then it is up to you to keep it burning. Once you know, you cannot unlearn the knowledge, and my hope is this book will change the way you, and every woman you meet, do business.

PART I

The Male Point of View

1

Who Are You?

How many of the following statements apply to you?

- You enjoy making people feel special at work.
- You bring baking or other culinary creations to share with coworkers.
- You track people's birthdays and anniversaries and touch base on those days to recognize the event.
- You like to plan company parties and events.
- You look to be seen as supportive and jump in with your sleeves rolled up to help out with company activities.
- You notice little things about what people like and track it so you can use that information later to surprise them with something.
- You prefer to sit quietly in the background and stay out of things unless called upon.
- You make suggestions on how people can get over colds.
- You believe that if someone wants something they should come to you and ask.

- You have decided that you don't have to be in the spotlight and you'll let the big mouths fight it out.
- You want to be seen as a necessary part of the team and someone who will focus on all the details.
- You think going out for drinks after work is a great way to build rapport.
- You look forward to company events, like Christmas parties and golf tournaments, where you can let your hair down and get to know colleagues on a more intimate level.
- You go on common vacations or mini retreats with coworkers.
- You have taken up golf so you can get deals going on the course.
- You have learned to like certain sporting events (hockey/baseball) so that you can be included in conversations.
- You have become very proficient at bluffing into conversations by nodding your head and smiling to keep the information going.
- You have found out the size of engine in your car so you can joke with the guys in the office.
- You have strong rules for how people get to interact with you and are quick to take offense if someone oversteps your boundaries.
- You believe that a good defense is a good offense.
- You enjoy having a strong personality and don't mind bowling over people who get in your way.
- You love the fact that you are referred to as a "force to be reckoned with."
- You will attack, if provoked, to show that you are serious about what you do.
- You believe that to be a leader you must exert your abilities to the group when it is misdirected.
- You like to manage people with an iron fist in a satin glove where you are tough on them, but considerate.

Commiserations! The more these statements fit you, the more you are undermining yourself to male colleagues in business. My guess is you're not closing specific deals. You're not getting invited to certain meetings. You're not being taken seriously by male colleagues. You're not moving ahead as quickly as you thought you would. Sound familiar?

You are sabotaging yourself. You now have your starting point for the rest of this book.

Reformation of an Alpha Male

Like most Alphas, I grew up in the shadow of my father. He was a strong, powerful ex-cop who ran construction companies most of his life. He was a man's man and was aggressive, driven, unstoppable, and successful. He was a hard act to follow as a kid. On summer vacations, I would get up with him, have breakfast, and then work around our house and yard most of the day—painting fences, running cables, weeding, mowing lawns. I would watch my friends ride by on their bikes, loving their time off, but I was only allowed to play with them after work and before dinner. Sometimes after dinner I would go out as well. I used to moan to my dad that it wasn't fair and that summer was for kids to have vacation. He would tell me that my friends and their parents simply lacked discipline and that he was raising me to be different. I would conspire with my friends for them to ask my dad if I could come out and play, and once in a while it would work, but basically my summers were for doing labor. I can remember being the only kid pleased about school starting again because it meant there was time to play at recess and lunch as well as after school.

My parents got divorced when I was in fifth grade and my mom and I moved away from my hometown to a larger city 90 minutes south. When my mom remarried three years later, I had my first insight into unions. My stepfather, one of the greatest men I've ever known, was a union guy. He had received many union contacts because his father was a union leader, and although hard working, he bought into the belief that the boss owed him something for his hard work. I was learning lessons as a young man from my Alpha Male father (who seemed to get everything) and my Beta Male stepfather (who seemed never to get enough). It was a confusing time, but I was very attracted to becoming more like my father because I liked to do things that cost money. I remember my father saying, "Fletts are good at everything it is worth being good at. The mud work can be hired out." Another lesson he taught me when I was young that has resonated through my life is, "If you want to be a leader, just assume leadership. Don't ask for it. People are weak and are uncomfortable when they don't have someone to follow. Fletts provide that leadership." You can imagine the ego that this created and continues to create.

The Grass Was Greener on the Other Side

When I was in 10th grade my mom and stepdad got me a job at the local A&W in Kamloops. It was a horrible job. I was a kitchen helper, which meant that I made sure all the condiments were filled up, the cooks had what they needed, I rotated the stock in the coolers, and so on. It was a horrible job, and the worst part was a team of demon women who worked in the kitchen. They had it in their minds that they would punish me for being a man because their husbands were assholes. They would pull pranks on me, get me to count pickles in 10 gallon pails (it only took me a week to figure out this was not necessary) and were generally nasty. My cool friends were working with their fathers in landscaping, construction, and other "manly" trades making $8–$10 an hour. I was a kitchen bitch making $3/hour and getting treated like a piece of crap.

I decided that I would step out and start my own company. I was 15 and thought that mowing lawns couldn't be that difficult. After querying my friends to see if their dads had jobs and finding out there were none, I decided to approach my mom and dad with a business proposition. At the dinner table that night, I allowed supper to start before making my deal. If my mom and dad would "spot" me $300 for a mulching lawnmower (then you don't have to pick up the clippings), I would pay them back for it by the end of summer. My mom looked at me with love in her eyes and said, "No!" I then looked to my stepdad, who always jumped on my side, and he said, "Chris, you should be happy you have a job." I was shocked. Parents were supposed to support their children, and my parents were dropping the ball. That's okay, I thought, I have an entrepreneurial father in Vancouver who will be so impressed with my idea he'll probably send up money the same day. I called my dad and ran the idea by him, and he said, "Chris, that's a great idea. You should do it, but I'm not going to help you. You don't want to be the guy whose dad built his company for him. Find a way to do it on your own." Are you kidding me? My entrepreneurial father wouldn't even bankroll his baby's dream. So I decided that my mom and stepdad, a little too socialist for my liking, would be targeted for a verbal attack every time we sat down for dinner until I wore them down. This took about two weeks of persistence until my mom, at breaking point, yelled across the table, "I will lend you the $300, but I want it back by the end of the summer and I want the lawnmower!" I think my mom thought that this would be too steep a price, but I jumped at it. What the hell was I going to do with a lawnmower after summer anyway? My stepdad and I went down to Sears to pick up the lawnmower and then I made flyers to circulate around the local trailer parks. I want you to know that Kamloops, where I grew up, is infested with trailer parks on the west side of the city. I'm talking thousands of trailers (aka: mobile homes). For $10 a week, I would mow a customer's 10-foot square lawn, weedwhack/trim the lawn, sweep out their carport, and take out their garbage. As you can imagine, trailer parks are inhabited by old people, and they saw this chubby 15-year-old entrepreneur coming around and couldn't resist. I should share with you that my only intention was to make more than $3/hour. At the end of my first week, I had 500 clients. I absolutely couldn't do the work. The city had a bylaw that noise was only tolerated from about 8 AM to 8 PM. I was working so frigging hard, I could barely keep up. I was making a fortune, but had to turn to my friends who were also working shitty jobs to come and help. The company grew through the summer, and I made more in three months than most lawyers were making in a year. I hid this fact from my parents so as to avoid any lectures, but I had a real taste of what it was like to live life large.

Getting Kicked Out of School

When I went to university, I started a business program, as my mother drilled into me the importance of a business degree. My father was somewhat so-so about the degree. He knew it might help me out, but I think he saw the entrepreneurial spark in me and was worried the business degree would spoil it. The school I went to was in Kamloops, and to put it politely, it didn't attract the very best business professors. Most I think had left some sort of post at a regional agricultural school and were teaching out of textbooks that were around when Warren Buffett was getting interested in the stock market. It was brutal. In every class, I would challenge the teacher, asking for real applications to what they were teaching me, but these challenged professors who had been hiding from the real world were rarely able to give an example different from the ones in the textbook. Let me be honest. I was a total pain in the ass. A big mouth, a disruption and bedsore to these people. My dad had said to me, "You are paying these people good money to teach you so don't just sit there and take notes, use them as advisers. Get them to answer the questions you want answered." I did—and sealed my fate with the university. While I was waiting to register for my third year (this was before automated registration by phone or online) the dean of student services came up and asked me for a chat. I didn't want to go and lose my place in line, but he told me that "after our discussion that wouldn't be an issue." I remember having no fear about having a conversation with him. I had been a shitty student and a problem in the class. I assumed he was kicking me out of school, and I thought, "It might be for the best. I can go start another company." Instead, he sat me down and said that three of the teachers on the business faculty refused to admit me to their classes, which were mandatory, and that my grades weren't good enough to transfer. He suggested that to avoid breaking my mother's heart I start either a science degree (don't think so) or an arts degree (McDonald's lobby duty). I told him that I would rather just leave, but he convinced me to try an arts degree. I ended up having exceptional teachers in history and philosophy who would let me study on tangents on the parts of history and philosophy I liked (the growth of American industry and the Japanese business model). As I walked by the business department and by faculty I knew, my contempt grew for those who told me that I wasn't right for business. I remember the president of the university saying to me just before graduation, "Chris, you better go to law school so you can make something of your life."

Building Think Tank

Out of school, I went right to work for BC Hydro, the provincial hydro energy company. The company was screwed. Everyone was power tripping on each other and backstabbing, and it didn't seem that anything got done efficiently. Everyone was so worried about keeping their job, they basically didn't move. They used to joke that when they were all standing around talking they were having a "safety meeting," because if nobody moved, no one could get hurt. I stayed there for six months and, after having my marketing plans either shot down or shelved, I quit at 1:26 PM on a Friday without any notice. My boss at the time smiled and said that he'd write me a great letter of recommendation. He said that I was too entrepreneurial to work in a Crown Corporation and should look at doing something on my own. I remember waiting for Jacqui to get home to tell her. She knew that I had been miserable, but was shocked that I had given no notice. She asked where I was going to work, and I told her that I would start my own company. She was supportive, but I know she was uncomfortable. Jacqui's family is not entrepreneurial, and starting a business in their minds is very risky. I thought to myself, "I have $6,000 in the bank, I just need a name and I'm good to go!" Sitting in my underwear the next morning watching CNN, I saw a group of young politicians who had been brought together to fix economic problems and they were referred to as a "think tank." I thought to myself, "Great name." At that moment, Think Tank Communications began business.

When I started, I wanted to do competitive research for cities looking to attract business to their areas. I was basically a headhunter, but rather than hunting people, I was hunting companies looking to move (or that could be convinced). I was 24 years old with a Bachelor of Arts degree and a six-month stint in a utility company. Extremely unattractive in the business market, I decided that I would have to be nimble, aggressive, and carve out my space in the market. I had back-to-back meetings for the better part of six months before the company started to grow. And once it started, it never looked back. Three months into the company, I was contacted by the other consultants in Kamloops (a bunch of washed-up government researchers) for a meeting. I remember being excited that we could explore ways of making money together. We met at the Denny's out on the highway, and the five of them sat down with me. One said, "Here's how it works. We all share work that comes in. We've been doing this a long time. You are new, don't have an MBA and bring little to the table. Stay out of our way and we might throw you some scraps." I stared at them, shocked. These "pikers," or pretenders, were going to tell me how things were going to work? I don't think so. I looked one dumb ass in the eyes and said, "Within a year many of you will be my bitches. Keep an eye open for my call." And with that I got up and walked out with hands carefully tucked in my pockets to conceal their shaking. I decided at that moment that I was going all in on this project and that I was either going to make it big or die trying.

With this scarcity mindset in my head (me against them), I worked the province like a madman. I traveled back and forth across the province making connections, getting work, and becoming a force. Within that first year, three of the five consultants did in fact do some subcontracting for me. My ego was feeding all the time, and I thought I was unstoppable. If a competitor dared get in my path, they'd either yield or I'd destroy them. It is surreal to look back on it now, but I can remember underbidding work to make sure that competitors with heavy overhead couldn't make payroll. I would help their employees become contractors, only to give them a small piece of work and never use them again. I even on occasion sent black roses to competitors when I'd get one of their key employees to quit or when I'd steal a contract from underneath them. I was the great white shark, top of the food chain, and I slept very well at night.

Good News, Bad News, Bad News

In 2000, I was asked to attend a conference in Calgary about economic development. I was the new kid on the scene and was creating a buzz with my ability to leverage government dollars for projects. Some called me the "Money Man," others called me "Firestarter." I liked to think the latter was because I got things going, but I think most used it because I created trouble. I had decided to make the almost 9-hour drive from Kamloops to Calgary, and my Dad in Vancouver asked to come so he could visit my sister who lives in Calgary. I had prepped all the things I was going to talk to him about (okay... brag to him about) on the trip. Men in my family are both animated and masters of one-upmanship. I picked up my dad in the Jeep, and we headed north from Vancouver. About two hours into the drive and after all the cursory small talk, I got ready to give my "presentation." My father stopped me and said, "I have good news, bad news, and worse news. Which do you want first?" I'm the type of guy who rips off the Band-Aid, so I said, "Give me the bad news." My dad looked at me and said, "I have cancer." I looked at him and—I'm ashamed to admit this now—thought, so? Fletts die of heart attacks, normally from stress and working very hard throughout our lives. Cancer was no big deal in my mind. "Cut it out," I said to him. "Go in on a Thursday afternoon, cut it out, take Friday and the weekend off, and you can be back at work on Monday." He looked at me and said, "It's worse than that." I thought he was being a pansy so I decided to change the topic. "What's the worse news? Do I have cancer?" I asked. "No," he said, "but you are an embarrassment to me and yourself." I believe an Alpha Male can only truly understand the devastation these words bring when you hear them from your mentor. We spend our whole lives trying to be like our fathers and then to surpass them. I felt that I had done both, and for him to tell me that he was embarrassed—it basically crashed my hard drive, if you know what I mean. I looked at him in utter shock. He said, "A man looks death in the face and replays all the tapes of his life. I did you a great injustice by encouraging you to do things the way I did. Now you are repeating my sins, only far greater. Your grandfather would be disappointed with both of us."

We pulled over to a rest stop and I was stunned. I went into one of the rest room's stalls and bawled my eyes out for about 10 minutes. My whole world had crumbled. I equate it to a dry piece of wood that you hit with an axe. It doesn't completely come apart, but you know there is a fracture right through it. That was my spine, soul, and ego all wrapped into one. After getting my shit together and returning to the car, my dad put his hand on my arm and said, "The good news is we have 18 hours of driving to make things right." Looking back, that was the first authentic conversation my dad and I had ever had on business. It was at that point that my transformation began.

When I returned home after the trip and many hours of talking to my father, I realized how poorly I had been doing things. The sad thing was all the Alpha Males I knew glorified me for being that way. I decided that if I was going to change, my business life would have to change. I would have to completely stop supporting things that were stuck in the old paradigm (the model that needs conflict, force, coercion, fear, and dominance) and embrace the new paradigm, but I didn't know what it was. In the following weeks, I started to dissect the business model and my role in it and realized that I had made things more difficult by trying to force coups rather than looking for business relationships that were easy. I rewrote the Think Tank mission statement. The existing one glorified us and all the great things we had done. The second one talked about the relationship my father had with his barber for 30 years, which was built on mutual respect and responsibility. I sent it to all my clients, and any of those who thought it funny, weak, or stupid were fired on the spot. That's right ... fired. In the new paradigm, service providers should actively fire clients that don't fit. About half of Think Tank's clients got fired, and in the six months after the mission statement went out our profits doubled.

This was when I started looking at our relationships with clients. We did extremely well with female clients and were constantly jockeying for position with male clients. Then I looked deeper at why female clients took so much longer to achieve while male counterparts flew right by them. Then I looked at success rates. Women succeed much more often than men, but take longer to do it. A majority of the work I did for the next three years was damage control when a female client would duff a business opportunity with an Alpha Male counterpart. I realized that men mentor men and women mentor women. I'd watch women dissect a situation with an Alpha Male but never ask for feedback from a man in a position to comment (i.e., another Alpha Male). And I'd watch Alpha Males deep-six women (destroy their careers – more on this later) and not even have the guts to own up to it. Could it be possible that women and men never talked authentically about how they do business? Women had the new model of business, but weren't drivers; men didn't fully understand the new model of business, but were used to being the pilot. Business was all screwed up, and the only people really succeeding were those who knew how both sides played the game. In my mind, I had been the black sheep of business. I had a bachelor of arts, not an MBA. I was young, lacked experience, and talked out of turn. I became successful by learning how to navigate around all the obstacles. Then I'd watch women assume that the obstacles were just part of the long road they had to walk. I realized that in order for business to move ahead, women had to be educated on how the Alpha Male works and invited to take the lead. Men built the glass ceiling, but women held it in place for the last 30 years. It was time to open that ceiling and let the new leadership lead. Read this book with a critical mind and challenge things you don't agree with while incorporating the things that make sense for you. This book will only be as good as how you use it. I have presented to 300 groups around the world, and it is my intention for this conversation to spread like a fire. I want women of all ages to know and agree or disagree. I'm not fussy on which they do. My responsibility is to make sure the conversation happens. When it does, my reformation is complete.

Alpha Male Terminology

Whenever I speak, I get asked to define the terms I'm using. I take it for granted that we all have the same vocabulary, but in reality the Alpha Male has slang of his own that is only really apparent to other Alphas. You may have heard some of these terms, but I want to clarify how I define them so you will know exactly what I'm talking about throughout this book.

Alpha Male

The Alpha Male is the top of the food chain. He is the one who brings in the deals and makes sure there is food on the table. He is the senior partner at a law firm. He is the top broker at a financial service firm. He is the guy whose name is all over all the apartment developments in a city. He is "the guy." He is the big player, the designated shooter, the all star. He is the guy who women want (those attracted to power) and the one who other men want to be. He is the great white shark of the ocean of business.

Pull the Trigger

Pull the trigger is a term Alphas use to refer to closing a deal. Everything about us has to do with dominance and what's more dominant than killing something. You've all heard men state that they are making a "killing" in the market. That they "killed on that deal." Pulling the trigger continues along these lines. We get something in our crosshairs (a client, deal, opportunity), and we dominate the opportunity by pulling the trigger. If you can't pull the trigger, you are destined to stay someone's bitch (property). Guys who are great at pulling the trigger are referred to as "shooters" or "designated hitters"—basically they are the ringer you put in the room when the deal has to close.

Ringer

The ringer is the secret weapon Alpha Male. He is the Alpha so smooth, impressive, powerful, and convincing that if someone sits down with him they are absolutely going to sign on the dotted line. Each Alpha likes to think of himself as a ringer, but in reality, we are specialists in particular situations. I'm very strong with women's groups while another ringer might be exceptional with law firms, small-cap start-ups, banks, and so forth. Think of the ringer as the major league baseball player you have playing on your community softball team. The advantage is so great that other teams should quiver in their shoes with the thought of him stepping on the field.

Pile-on

Remember in school there was the nerdy kid who someone would trip and the rest of the group would pile on top of them? Some people called it "dog piling." Well, in business, Alphas look to identify pile-ons who will do our work for us. We like to take the lead on projects, but then we don't do the work because that part isn't a lot of fun. We like to hunt up new work, not do the work we have. A pile-on can refer to an actual subordinate who has to do what we say, but it usually refers to helpers who don't have to answer to us but can do our work just the same. We need pile-ons because we leave things till the last minute and then face the terror of not having something done on time (missing our goals is a no-no and a big embarrassment for an Alpha in front of other Alphas). Instead, we go fishing for pile-ons. I walk out into the main area and start looking for someone to do my work. I normally do this on a Friday afternoon if my work is due on Monday. Here's an example:

Step 1: (Talking to myself, but loud enough for others to hear.)

"Oh man, I have so much work to do and it has to be done by Monday or I'm screwed ..."

(Then I wait. If nothing, I take it to Step 2, but I'm almost always guaranteed at least one pile-on who wants to be helpful.)

"It's my wife and my anniversary this Saturday but I think she will understand if we postpone it for a week so I can get this stuff done ... "

(This normally flushes out all the pile-ons who are wives, have met my wife, or are trying to protect me from getting in trouble at home. This normally is good for at least two or three pile-ons. If I haven't got enough pile-ons to take all my work, then I go to Step 3.)

"The hardest part about this weekend is it is my son's baseball tournament and I promised him I wouldn't miss any more games, but I really need to keep things good at work so I think he will understand. My wife can go in my place ... "

(This normally flushes out the rest of the pile-ons. The mothers, the grandmothers, the women with little brothers—anyone who thinks of my little son crying because I've broken another promise to him.)

Now that I have alleviated my three-foot pile of paperwork that has to get done by Monday to my various pile-ons, I'm free to take the weekend off. I have identified the women who are trying to be helpers, those who are trying to keep my marriage in good shape and those who are trying to make me a better dad. Now I have my crew that I can delegate work to. But it gets worse from there for my pile-ons. Not only do I have absolutely no intention of ever helping them when they need to get something done (just get really busy with make-believe projects when they come for help), but I now share with my Alpha Male colleagues that you are a pile-on and the best approach to get you to help (she's a basic helper, a marriage saver, or a parental supporter). Now my fellow Alphas are free to play with me on the weekends while pile-ons complete our work.

Boat Anchor

A boat anchor is the lowest of the low to an Alpha Male. This is a person who makes you feel like you are swimming with a boat anchor tied around your neck when you're doing business with him or her. This is someone who is in your circle of business and basically wants you to carry the relationship. They will meet with you, ask your advice, but continue to under perform or simply not perform at all. They have all the reasons in the world why they aren't successful, but basically they suck. They lack ability but know someone who is keeping them in place. We've all seen the kid with the water wings on in the pool. Daddy has a hold of the back of their trunks yet they truly believe they are swimming. We all know if Daddy lets go of the trunks, that little bugger is going to sink like a brick. The boat anchor is a man or woman who does business like that kid swims. Look good if they are held up, but they are toast when left to their own accord. Alphas report boat anchors to each other like truckers report speed traps. Beware, beware, beware! If you are a boat anchor, it is only a matter of time before some Alpha deep sixes you and then you'll be out of the game. If you can't perform, find a job that doesn't require ability and do that.

Finder/Minder/Grinder

Everyone in business gets classified by one of these three terms. The Finder is someone who can find work, bring in opportunities, pull the trigger, build sales funnels, and basically make sure there is food on the table. The Minder is the manager—someone who ensures the work gets done, but doesn't have the ability to hunt it. The Grinder is the sorry sap who does the work for which the company is getting paid. If dad is the hunter who kills the chicken for soup, he is the Finder. Mom puts together the ingredients, makes sure the pot is on the stove and everything is cooking. She is the Minder. The kid, who has to pluck the chicken, peel the potatoes, cut the carrots, and so on, is the Grinder.

If we look at it from a true business example, you will see where Alphas get our inflated, but often earned, egos. A law firm has Alphas running the firm as managing partners. These hotshots may be good lawyers (technicians), but they are even better at bringing in business. One or two of them might be worth 50 percent or more of the firm's business. They take clients for supper, to hockey games, golf rounds, 'boys' weekends' in Vegas. They romance, attract, and pull the trigger on clients and their work. Their actions ensure that there is money coming into the firm in the form of retainers. Once the Finder (Alpha) brings in the work, someone has to make sure that the work gets done. Normally this is either a junior partner or a senior associate. They take the file and look at what needs to get done. They break down the steps and set time and other measurements to make sure it is done on time. These are the Minders or managers of the file. Then these Minders look to the lowly little associates working in the basement next to the Coke machine and give them the work to do. These individuals are the Grinders, and it is their role to make sure the work gets done. We can all agree that each component is important. If the Grinders don't do the work, nothing can get billed. If the Minders don't make sure the work gets done, there can be price overruns, scheduling issues, and other challenging situations. But to the Alpha (Finder), if he doesn't do his job, the rest is moot. The other two are only important once he has done his job. The livelihoods of everyone rest on his ability to pull the trigger, and that's why he is at the top of the food chain.

Mud

Mud is a term Alphas use for people below us. Grinders and Minders are often referred to as mud because they don't know what the good life is or they don't want it. Alphas have two sayings that we use all the time with each other and laugh every time we hear them as if it was the first.

"Whoever said that money was the root to all evil didn't have any," and "Money can't buy happiness, but I can park my mega yacht right beside happiness and that's good enough for me."

Mud can also be used as a synonym for "shit." Here are some examples we use in everyday business:

- "Toyotas are mud."
- "They are flying mud class" (coach class on an airplane). We actually refer to the curtain they pull across the isle between business and coach as a "mud flap."
- "That is mud work. Give it to a pile-on."
- "Your sales team is mud. You need some ringers in there to pull the trigger."

You can see by these examples that our Alpha vocabulary works very well when used together. Mud is the low point of anything. It's the dollar store, it's traveling by Greyhound, it's the car your Grandma left you in her will.

Earner

This is a subjective term and has a quantifiable definition depending on the Alpha using it. Because we are always trying to get into more and more exclusive positions, we use the term Earner to define anyone who makes a lot of money. When an Alpha makes $100,000 a year, in his mind, an Earner makes at least $100,000 a year. When he makes $200,000 a year, an Earner is no longer someone who makes $100K, but now it is someone making $200K a year. This definition continues to grow with him as he makes more money. Think of Lance Armstrong when he is attacking a stage in a race. Everyone in the pack is a cyclist, but when he zips up his jersey and starts to pump those legs, he becomes the real cyclist and the rest of the pack are just guys out for a ride. We Alphas like to use Earner as a measurement as long as we are in the group. If my friends think $250K a year is Earner level and I'm only making $185K, I am not happy. This is a topic of conversation whenever Alphas sit down with each other. The discussion of what constitutes an Earner is a way we can take the temperature to see how much money everyone is making.

Bank or Banker

These two related terms basically refer to those who are extremely wealthy. We define rich as someone with a lot of money. We define wealth as having resources that continue to grow and grow all the time. A man can be rich if he makes $100K a year, has a nice house and car paid off, and vacation properties. A man is wealthy if he can sit in bed all day and still make a fortune. When a man makes an enormous amount of money, we refer to him as a banker. He has so much money coming in, it would be difficult for him to spend it. He in effect becomes a banker. We refer to the term "bank" if someone is making a lot of money. Here is how we use the slang:

- "Your ideas makes a lot of sense, why don't you connect with a group of bankers and see if you can get them on board to finance it for a couple of points (percentage of the deal)."
- "I am making serious bank off that deal. It just keeps coming in and coming in. There is no way for me to spend what is coming in this year unless I buy a fleet of houses."

A banker is truly the upper echelon of Alpha Males. I know guys who have $4 million lines of credit for business opportunities they come across, all personally guaranteed. That's "bank."

Mouth

A mouth is a woman who can't shut up. She promises that she will keep things confidential, but it always gets back that she talked. When confronted, she acts surprised, "not realizing that everything was a secret." This is a woman who is either quickly deep sixed or is simply left out to hang. My colleague Liz always says, "Time is longer than rope." Give people enough of either and they'll hang themselves.

Snitch

A snitch is a male version of the mouth. He can't be trusted, is almost always a Beta Male, and tries to use information as a currency to leverage favors. This is a guy who will have a horrible professional life because Alphas will attack him for sport, for retribution, or simply because he has no place in the business world. Alphas work on a code of honor with each other, which Betas and most women do not share. An Alpha never screws over a buddy. An Alpha never dates a friend's ex. An Alpha never betrays a trust, especially when he has given his word that he won't. We have a saying in business: "There are two types of people who get murdered in prison: child molesters and snitches."

In business, if any Alpha identifies a snitch, we will take time out of whatever we are doing to make his life so difficult he will think the hand of God Himself is crushing his career. In police forces they refer to it as the "thin blue line," in the military they refer to it as "foxhole confessions," in organized crime they refer to it as "dinner table talk," and in business circles we call the discussions between two equals as "a conversation of non-disclosure." Break the code in any of these examples and the consequences are both swift and severe.

Bitch

Women all assume that when a man is intimidated, disturbed, frustrated, or angered by a strong woman, she is referred to as a *bitch*. Nothing could be further from the truth. I can count on one hand how many times in the last year I have heard a woman referred to as a bitch in a business setting. In the last 48 hours from writing this, I can count on both hands and both sets of toes how many times I've heard a man referred to as a bitch. Alphas use the term "bitch" to suggest someone is submissive to us. Examples:

- "Tom, I heard you blew that deal. If you want, you can come and type letters for me at the office. I think you'd make a good office bitch, especially now that we know you can't close deals."
- "Dave, now that I'm making double what you are, would you like to become my personal bitch? You can get my coffee, shine my shoes –you know, all the things you are good at."

- "Did you see Kevin blow that deal? What a little bitch."
- "Bitch up!" (This translates to "suck it up.")
- What do you mean you can't come to the conference? Your wife doesn't want you to go? Quit being her bitch, bitch."
- "Come on guys. We need to close that deal. Do you want those sniveling bitches to take our clients?

We use this term to spur each other on or to slam the competitors that we are positioning against in deals. Men use this term as an acknowledgment of pecking order—no Alpha wants to be referred to as a bitch . . . ever.

Piker

A piker is a pretend Alpha or an Alpha who hasn't reached the highest levels of accomplishment yet. He wears a fake Rolex. He rents a house he tells people he owns. He leases a car nicer than he can afford to buy. He acts like he knows scotches, cigars, and watches. He is a poser. When accomplished Alphas get wind that a piker is "playing the role," they all make him their bitch. They talk about his car lease payments, ask him how it feels to pay off someone else's mortgage, and if he is ever worried about washing his hands with his shitty knock-off watch on. "Piker" can also refer to a guy who can't close. He might get up to bat (presentation) but then he strikes out. Alphas pride ourselves in the ability to close juicy deals. Pikers just screw up the gene pool.

Deep Six

This is the process we use to sabotage your credibility and your career. It comes from underwater (you rarely see it coming), and it has a devastating effect on your position in business. We'll discuss this later in the book.

Pecking Order

Simply put, the pecking order is how people rank in comparison to others. Alphas are at the top, followed by Beta Males (easily controlled by Alphas), then Alpha Females (driven), then Beta Females (supporters and often pile-ons). Finally, at the bottom of the pecking order are the Mouths, Pikers, and Snitches.

Henning

This is how we refer to women's groups that are meant to facilitate networking, yet all that happens is women talk to the same people as at the last event and don't build any business. Women at events like this are like hens—clucking away, rarely about anything important, snuggling up to each other, giggling, making sure everyone is included, talking about your lives, and getting absolutely nothing accomplished. You may argue I'm making a huge generalization, but ask yourself how much business you have received from attending networking events? Is it more or less than your male counterparts? Women are busy networking while Alphas are developing powerful networks. There's a big difference!

Breeders

These are women who are continuously on maternity leave. Women like this cause major disruptions to business because they don't take responsibility for the effect it has on their business responsibilities. Women walk into their boss' office and drop the bomb: "I'm pregnant! Be happy for me!" Then she walks out and thinks about what she is going to do with her year off. The boss needs to find either someone to take over the role for a year (hence reducing his pool of pile-ons) or find someone who will come in on contract. This is not going to be popular, but I need to say it: *If you are going to have kids, don't make it anyone else's problem. Take responsibility for everything, including your workload!* If you go to your boss with a plan on how his life won't get harder by you being a breeder, he will be surprised, shocked, happy for you, and you will come back in the exact same position you left at (in the pecking order). If your offspring makes his life harder, he is going to look for a way to deep-six you before you get pregnant again.

Business Models over the Last Fifty Years

There has been lots of talk about how the economy has changed since World War II. There have been books written about women entering the workforce, the atomic family, working parents and the loss of the family compact, the DINK (Double Income, No Kids) scenario, and the like. What we haven't looked at is exactly what is happening now in office gender politics, how the last 30 years have led up to it, and why the Alpha Male still guards the yard but has lost his teeth in the current model. I want to share with you my take on what has happened and how I see now being the start of a paradigm of business that could last for a very, very long time.

1980s

My mom and dad were both in real estate during the boom of the 1980s. They were putting deals together left, right, and center. My mother sold 17 houses in one month, and my dad was penning deals on a daily basis. The '80s were all about extravagance, indulgence, and excess. It was about driving a big car, living in a big house, and having the big job. The movie "Wall Street" epitomized what business looked like. I remember watching that movie every weekend when I was a kid from age 11 till I was about 17. I had to buy new copies when the old ones wore out. Gordon Gecko, played by Michael Douglas, is the definitive Alpha Male. He works in the big office, putting big deals together. He is much too busy to leave the office and get fitted for suits, so his tailor comes and measures him as he is on his headset in his office putting deals together. He has the best seats in restaurants, the best apartment, and a huge staff. Other men try just about everything to do business with him. Gordon set the tone for this generation with his statement, "Greed is good!" God, I loved that man and spent much of my youth trying to mimic the way he acted. Our family didn't help the situation. My mom drove a new Cadillac. They started work at 7AM and normally got home around 9 PM. We were a powerful family. When my mom had open houses, my job was to have LEGOs out in the specified play area, and as soon as the prospective family would come in, I'd introduce myself to the kids and invite them to play with me. If parents weren't being bothered by their kids, they'd have more time to look at the house and for my mom to "set the hook." The prospective parents would even start to imagine little Jimmy and Becky in the playroom enjoying their new home. My parents were part of the '80s machine that really set the pecking order in society for decades to come. This was a very good time for Alpha Males and basically served as their framework for how the world should work.

I remember my Dad telling me that the process of becoming an Alpha Male was to get into university, get an exceptional job, and then around 40 you either started your own company (once you understood business principles) or started your climb up the ivory staircase to senior management. I remember being confused as a kid as to what the fuss was about with having a key to an executive bathroom! The '80s were the heyday for Alphas, and they thrived in it and believed that it would never end. The model that their fathers and their fathers' fathers had worked to create was finally a reality. I can't count the number of days when my parents would pick me up from school and we'd immediately hit the mall. We would buy everything we wanted, and in retrospect I wonder if we did it because we enjoyed it or because of what the activity represented. I knew at that point that if I followed that model I would be rich, powerful, and envied. But, that model didn't last.

1990s

In the 1990s new technology came about and, all of a sudden, 15-year-olds in their basements and garages started developing applications and concepts that made them millionaires overnight. As these shifts started to happen, the Alpha Males held their collective breath, assuming that this was simply a blip on the screen and the market would correct it. Boy, were they wrong! Technology companies started getting financed and dominating the stock exchanges. Twenty-one-year-old CEOs were traveling the globe with their venture capitalist backers in search of deals for software and technologies that only existed in theory. They were taking over expensive office space in the world's business centers and living the good life. The Alpha Male contingent watched these would-be Bill Gates-types and realized that the model had fundamentally changed. The Alpha Males had worked so hard to get their model to finally work perfectly only to have Junior and his laptop take it all away. There was only one option: leave corporate and become venture capitalists or senior advisers to these new companies!

Many of the Alpha Males who had followed the recipe of success divested out of that model and joined the technology revolution. They cashed in their 401Ks and Registered Retirement Savings Plans and invested in these start-up companies. They left the 6 to 9 (the Alpha Male's version of the 9 to 5) and sat on advisory boards, took on new roles in the start-ups with new titles (VP of People, VP of Creative Investment, etc.) and made a conscious decision to carve out a space in this new model they could dominate.

Lots of money went around in the '90s, and although the Alphas who got on board were successful, I think many of them felt a certain level of contempt for other men, their juniors by 20-plus years, enjoying the same or higher level of success. Alpha Males believe that you earn your place at the dinner table, and many of these young men hadn't invested in business school, hadn't put in their time in middle management, and in most cases, weren't Alpha Males. These technology guys are almost always made up of Beta Males who hate conflict, just love the challenge of the work (not entirely driven by money), and think that their company is their baby (Alphas build companies to sell). Betas don't have the kill mindset and think that Alphas are too aggressive. Alphas hate guys like this because it makes them think of the weakest version of themselves and this disgusts them. This was a tough pill for the Alpha Male group to swallow, only slightly softened by the amount of money they were making in their new positions.

The market correction that the Alphas thought would happen immediately took almost a decade to arrive, and when it did, there were casualties. The Alphas, assuming it was the new gold rush, dropped all of their best practices that had made them successful (competitive research, letters of intent from prospective buyers, using creative financing rather than their own money) and jumped into the water without knowing if it was safe. It proved the description that Alphas "shoot, ready, aim" rather than "aim, ready, shoot." In his excitement about this being the "next best thing," the Alpha abandoned all the tools that helped him build his various successes. The Alpha even forgot to forge his Plan B (his backup plan in case things go sideways), which forced him to fully commit to this new model and roll the dice. Most of the technology companies that developed had no business model. Many didn't have business plans; rather, they used investment prospectuses. They had no clients, no partners, and no established sales channels. They were simply ideas that were overvalued, and when the dot com bomb hit, it was like dry wood in a fire. Everything went up. Only the giants, like Amazon, survived. Many over-vested companies, like Nortel, sustained enormous damage and sentenced an entire generation to a delayed retirement as their resources disappeared.

Alphas, although bleeding profusely, put on their game faces and decided to revisit the old model of business using the best of new technology. E-mail, videoconferencing, and online presentations were all new tools in their business development arsenal. They combined their old practices of business development with technological advances that allowed them to "work the world." They cut and slashed through new markets with the same vigor and contempt as before, remembering that the world was big and they could walk through it as they liked without consequence. The other great thing they discovered about technology was that you didn't have to meet your customers. You could hit them with e-mail, video conferencing, address their concerns through automated call centers and bill them automatically.

What the Alphas forgot was that the same technology that allowed them to work the world also allowed the world to talk to itself. The "rape and pillage" and "slash and burn" mindsets of business development now followed them wherever they went. If you screwed someone in Paris, they could let all their affiliates know in the stroke of a keyboard and click of a mouse. Bloggers were commenting without consequence on what companies were doing, and the world of business was simply a broadcast e-mail away. Alpha Males would feel the results of their actions now in a matter of seconds rather than in months or years as before. The model of business was set to change yet again, and the Alpha wasn't sure of his next step.

2007

Because the world has grown even smaller, and technology has made things easier in some respects (like online learning) and harder in others (like that damn automated operator when you call your telephone service), a new model of business is needed to keep customers loyal. I believe that this new model started to flourish in early 2001 and continues to dominate business today. The new model, which I will henceforth refer to as the *new paradigm*, is based on integrity, authenticity, and relationships. The integrity part means doing what is right, authenticity means delivering what is promised, and the relationship means knowing the person or people you are doing business with. This is how women have been doing business for the last 50 years, but the Alpha Males have chastised them for it because they felt women spent too much time caring. But the truth is the new model is perfectly suited for women; the market has corrected itself after 50 years of doing things almost right, but never completely right. This isn't about employment equity or fair wages—it's bigger than that. Women are now in a position to lead because theirs is the only model that works in the new global business environment.

It always frustrated me to watch women asking men for equality in business. By definition, one cannot be equal if one has to ask for it. Today, however unreasonably, it is still men doling out the privileges. Women must learn to assume power and show the world that they are a force to be reckoned with in business as well as in life.

Alpha Males are quietly looking to women for guidance in business, but to an Alpha Male asking for help is the equivalent of saying, "I'm too weak to figure it out on my own." So, they quietly sit back and observe, but in reality it will take honest conversation for men to master what women have known for decades: Caring about the people you do business with is not only important, it is imperative. As I say in my seminars, the plane of business is on autopilot. Men don't know how to fly it, and no one has shared with women that they are the perfect pilots for this new paradigm. My intention is for the conversation we start here to continue on between individuals, teams, companies, and economies. It isn't about men giving women an "equal" chance. It is about women stepping into the light and taking control of a model that only they can manage. Alpha Males aren't going to go away, but those in my generation realize that the change has happened, and we have a lot more respect for women (due to having strong mothers) than my father's generation did. Even with this respect, Alpha Males are Alpha Males, and we have certain drivers and frustrations in business that once women know they won't forget. I get asked all the time at keynotes if I think women should act more "Alpha Male"-like. Absolutely not! If you do, you will blow the opportunity to lead and to educate us (men) on the proper way of doing sustainable business.

I like to equate the new paradigm for women to traveling to Paris. In Canada, we study French as a government regulation from when we are in elementary school right through to university. I never really enjoyed French and tried to learn it, but never did very well. I basically passed each course, but wouldn't say I was able to communicate at any exceptional level. In 2003, I was in Quebec City and was trying to use my French out of respect. I went into a coffee shop in the old city and there was a large male tourist looking for a cup of coffee. He asked in English, and the woman behind the counter said, "Pardon?" Then he yelled his order, I guess assuming that if he raised his voice, she would instantly understand English. She just looked at him with a blank look on her face. He stormed out without his coffee and undoubtedly without a fond experience of Quebec City. I was up next. I went up and asked in butchered French for a latte. She looked at me, and I was ready for the expected "Pardon," but instead she smiled and said in perfect English, "Would you like to know the correct way to say that in French?" I nodded, and she walked me through the phrase. Then she happily got me my coffee, walked it over to the table, and took my money. I was totally perplexed by how rough she was on the first guy and so helpful to me. Then it dawned on me. The first guy expected her to act in a way that would benefit him, whereas I had reached out to her in an attempt (poorly) to speak in her language. I took one step toward her, and she took 10 toward me. Her assumption was that, as an English speaker, I was going to expect her to speak in my language rather than in hers. Can you imagine someone coming from a city outside of North America and getting miffed at you if you didn't speak Dutch or Cantonese?

The same holds true for communicating with Alpha Males. We have learned in our personal lives that to be successful with women we must consider how we say things to them. We know how to translate our thoughts so they deliver the message we want to get across to our female counterpart. For women to build business and relations with men in business, they might consider speaking to Alpha Males in the language men understand. If you approach a man this way, at first he will be shocked, then bewildered, impressed, and finally will want to engage with you on a deeper level because you aren't "one of those girls." "One of the girls" is the default position that all women start at. We make assumptions that we believe hold true for most women (stereotypes), and we manage our relationships with you with these in mind. When you start to debunk these beliefs we have about you, it makes us take a closer look at you. When I'm working with a woman, these are my fundamental expectations:

1. At some point in the relationship, she will try to be cute to get something she wants (you call it feminine charm, we call it an inability to negotiate properly).
2. She will get upset, cry, get angry, be hurt, or crumble if we act against her in a business transaction.
3. She can't be told anything privately that we don't want the whole world to know.
4. She will expect me to know what is on her mind and will think that I need to work hard to be in a relationship with her.
5. She will try to ride my coattails as much as I will let her.
6. I will be responsible for pulling most triggers (closing deals), but she will want me to share credit with her.
7. She believes that I will take care of her and take a bullet for her if it comes to it.
8. She will seek counsel from her female friends when I do something she doesn't understand (and that's where she will spill her guts on what we are trying to keep secret).
9. She will seek counsel from her boyfriend, husband, dad, or brother, and these irrelevant people will be giving her strategies that will just mess up the situation.
10. It is more likely than not that she and I will have conflict at some point and I will have to deep-six her. I prepare myself for this

when we first start working together, and I keep her at an arm's distance so when I do it I don't have any feelings of guilt about it.

When a woman enters my business life, I internally nod to myself that the previously mentioned are all points of danger of engaging with her. When she does things that are the opposite of my expectations (i.e., she doesn't take things personally in front of me, she doesn't give me peanut gallery advice from her husband or father, she closes deals on her own, she keeps things confidential, and she understands that everyone is responsible for eating only what they kill) I will be pleasantly surprised and will take her out of the "one of those girls" category and start to consider her an equal colleague.

When I was in Quebec, I didn't have to become French to attempt speaking their language. You do not have to become an Alpha Male in order to communicate with them in a way that they understand. I could decide to always speak English in foreign countries, the same way you could decide to continue speaking the language of women, and both of us will likely get most of what we want some of the time. I believe, however, that if we each make some effort to speak and act in a way that gets our message across to the intended audience, while ensuring *our integrity is intact*, we will have a deeper and less arduous task in life and business.

2

The Many Business Types

I am what the world would call a Young Alpha Male. I am a hunter in the true sense of the word. I take pride in eating what I kill. This is how Alpha Males describe building business. I laugh in the face of obstacles because they give me the chance to prove to the world that I can't be stopped. When I'm in a room, I feel superior to everyone else. My ego, however delicate, is my power core. I use it to make all my decisions, and it influences all my actions. In this book, I will dissect the Alpha Male in western business. I will pull back the curtain and share with you what I think, why I do what I do, how I see things, and most important why I succeed. I have learned many tricks from a long list of Alpha mentors who at one point or another for selfish reasons decided I was worthy.

Everyone the Alpha Male meets is placed into the pecking order in his mind. We arrange people like a little boy would his hockey cards, placing the ones with the most value up front and those with little value at the end. I'm going to take you through the different categories of the Alpha Male's pecking order.

The Alpha Male

The Alpha Male is the great white shark of business. He is at the top of the food chain and swims around his ocean looking for things to eat. Much like the great white, if he stops swimming he dies (or at least feels like he is dying). The Alpha Male is the guy who closes deals, who sets up alliances that make money, and who is almost entirely driven by money and power. A man is born either an Alpha or a Beta Male. That's not to say that Alpha Males always come from Alpha Male fathers. Instead, some men have inherent traits that position them to become Alpha Males. The Alpha is driven, he is goal-focused, he enjoys conflict, he is greatly concerned with position in life, he doesn't like to follow others' rules, he likes to try the impossible, and he will accept nothing but the best for himself and his family. The Alpha Male is the reason deals have been done over the last 200 years. Alpha males generally are not dangerous in business unless you undermine them or attack their credibility. Instead, they are simply focused on goals and approach business like a runaway truck—you are either in it or under it. I like to think of Alpha Males as two types: those who have something to prove (often younger) and those who have been to war and lived to talk about it (older ones). The younger ones are great running partners, and the older ones are great mentors. I will describe each one so you understand how they act and so you can recognize the Beta Males who are pretending to be Alpha Males.

Young Alpha

Young Alphas are normally between the ages of 18–40, although you can find them a bit older in some cases. The young Alpha is happiest when he is pulling the trigger, putting in the long hours, presenting to large crowds, and making lots and lots of dough. He is focused on creating a name for himself, developing a bulletproof network, and having as many kills (business deals) as possible under his belt. He likes the cars, toys, watches (all of which we will talk about in later chapters), and he is all about the show.

He often hangs around with other young Alphas and will have a handful of older Alphas that he learns from, brags to, and leverages to get him into bigger games. He lives in a constant state of fear that he will be found out to be a fraud in business. He often bites off more than he can chew, and his mantra is "I don't need to know everything. I just need the ability to find something out before a client finds out that I don't know." He carefully contemplates his father's life and decides what he will do differently and what he will model.

He wants to do everything quicker, faster, and more profitable than anyone before him, and he craves celebrity and respect from people he has never met. He wants to be the topic of conversation at dinner tables. If anything gets in his way, he gnashes his teeth and declares war immediately. He craves to be proven in battle, yet is constantly concerned that someone bigger will take a run at him. Every month he looks at how much he is making, how much he could have made, and where he sits in the pecking order of the people he knows. He is simultaneously his own biggest cheerleader and most devastating critic. No one can drive a young Alpha harder than he drives himself. He lays in his king-sized bed each night deciding what he could have done differently, replaying his successes and failures, and wondering, "Is tomorrow the day when they find out I'm in over my head?"

A young Alpha becomes an old Alpha not necessarily by the passing of years but by accruing accomplishments. Once he has enough money and accolades under his belt, he can start to breathe a bit. He starts to cherry pick his deals and finds, in doing so, that better deals start to come. The old Alpha is what all Alphas aspire to be.

Old Alpha

The old Alpha is a more relaxed version of the young. He is no less driven, but he has learned that leverage is the best way to get business done. As the young takes pride in how much work he can do, the old takes pride in how much work he can have others do for him. The young makes great money by himself; the old has many people make him lots of money. The young is in the office at 5:30 AM; the old is taking clients on his boat, to a hockey game, or to Vegas for a fight. The old looks at the young and remembers the price he paid to get in the big game, and the young looks to the old for inspiration to take his game up a level.

I find that old Alphas are like old dogs lying on the porch. They have done the hunting, the fighting, and the marking of territory. They now want to relax a bit, confident in the safety of their kingdom. The young

Alpha is like the puppy. Full of piss and vinegar, he runs around barking in the air, checking things out, and chewing on things. He will run over to the old dog, chew on his ear a bit, bark at him, and follow him when he goes somewhere. I think we act very similarly in business. Many of the old Alphas I know or have known in business were lighthouses for my practice. I would go out on my own, but always kept an eye on where they were and what they were doing. I navigated by where they were and what they were doing. I'd brag to them about what I was doing, assuming that I was the only person ever to have done that, only to hear that they did the same thing about a dozen years ago. The old Alpha keeps the young in line. My friend and mentor Alvin Con of Intel was a great example of this. I was building a fledgling and failing technology company, and I'd follow him into meetings where I'd watch him hunt. I would sit quietly and observe what he said and what he didn't. He would give me glimpses of what the big dog table looked like. I can remember sitting in on deals where Hitachi, Intel, and various other multinationals were talking about moving into the Canadian market. They would estimate how much gear a university would need, how many servers and broadband a city could use, and so on. These guys were talking in the millions and tens of millions of dollars worth of new business. Then they would strategize about how to enter the markets to make sure that everyone was included. It was like visualizing Winston Churchill in his war room during WWII. Alphas endorse each other (which we will talk about later) and get each other into games that selfishly benefit them. Here's one example:

Alvin and I were sitting over lunch at Milestones one Friday and I was complaining about the challenge of being taken seriously in technology with limited knowledge. I had two partners, a chief financial officer and chief information officer, who were managing development and operations, and my responsibility was to find deals for us to get into. Alvin and I were discussing how to position a deal where we would service a local university by providing wireless Internet access everywhere on campus. As we brainstormed ideas, I came up with some great plans and Alvin asked me to develop a white paper (a discussion paper around a specific deal). When it was complete, I brought copies for the companies we were partnering with and went over it. Alvin told me to keep an eye on a couple of the people at the table who he thought were opportunists. He told me that my idea was my buy in to the table. Long story short, one of the people at the table took my idea to competing providers and put together a $300 million deal. I was crushed, and a week afterwards Alvin and I reviewed the post mortem over cigars. I was in a bad place, and Alvin looked at me and smiled. He said, "Pal, don't focus on the fact that you had a deal scooped out from underneath you. Focus on the fact that you are 26 and you came up with a workable deal to the tune of $300 million. Next time you'll get a non-disclosure agreement and then you'll make bank."

Weeks later I was still complaining about not being taken seriously in the technology sector and Alvin said to me, "You want to be taken seriously? Okay, I'm hosting an Intel Wireless Technology Conference this weekend. I will put you on the speakers list to talk about customer service in call centers. You and I both know you don't know shit about that topic, but the question is, can you learn enough in three days to impress people that are going to be there and not embarrass me? If yes, you are in. If no, I don't want to hear any more bellyaching. This is your chance. Do you want it?" I looked at him and replied, "Yes!" I shook his hand and thanked him and walked out of the restaurant. Within a few steps, the terror sank in. In 72 hours, I was going to be talking in front of 100 technology barons about how wireless call centers managed Tier 1 and 2 support. I was screwed. On top of embarrassing myself, Alvin would deep-six me and I'd be toast. I quickly ran to a local bookstore chain, bought "Wireless Networking for Dummies" and consumed the book. I can't remember what I did to prepare nor how the event went, but Alvin came up afterwards, shook my hand, told me "well done," and then got out of the way as guys came up from the major technology companies asking me for a business card and giving me theirs. He had reinforced what my dad had always said: "You don't need to know everything, you just need to know more than your clients. And if you don't know, it's your job to find out faster than they can find out you don't know what you are talking about."

Before meeting Alvin I thought $50,000 deals were impressive. Then he would tell me about $100 million deals he was piecing together. We would sit together at our cigar club with other Alphas (young and old) and relive our hunting stories of the week. Alvin and I had a lunch and cigar date every Friday for a year, and I learned more in that period of time than I had at any time before or since. I've had a lot of Alpha Male mentors (and many Alpha Female mentors as well).

These are some of the things I've learned from the guys:

1. Success is yours for the taking. If you want it, you need to claim it.
2. Leadership is given to those who take complete responsibility.
3. The world drives over weakness.

4. No one honors someone who pulls punches. If you are going in, go all in.
5. Find the game, learn the game, play the game, and dominate the game.
6. I don't have to choose. I can have everything I want the way I want it.
7. If I don't like the rules, change them.
8. Be prepared to challenge everything I think is unjust to me.
9. Ask for what I want.
10. For those who get in my way, invite them onto the steamroller or roll over them.
11. Mediocrity always attacks those who excel.
12. It is lonely at the top.
13. A man who lives a life without passion lives a life not worth leading.
14. There is an art to putting deals together. Like anything it needs to be practiced daily.

Alvin died a few years ago of cancer. I remember seeing him in the hospital a few months before he died and hearing that the doctor had told him to get his affairs in order. I told Alvin that the doctor could go fuck himself and that he had to fight. As he got more ill, I stayed away from him. I don't know why. In judo, when an opponent is injured you kneel facing away from them to give them time to be cared for. I was brought up that when a man is hurting you give him space, but I gave him too much and didn't get a chance to say goodbye.

When I got the call that he had died, I was walking up a staircase to give a business presentation. I sat on the staircase in a daze, feeling like the wind had been knocked out of me. It has been rare in my life that I have felt pain that great, and sitting there I just wanted to go home and go to bed. Alvin was the kind of guy who loved the deal. He loved his own deals, he loved helping others in deals, and he loved hearing about deals. I went up and did my presentation as he would have wanted it and then drove home and stayed in bed for three days. My great mentor had died, and a piece of me died with him.

Now as an older Alpha Male, and out of respect for the gifts Alvin gave me, I work with young Alphas and nudge them when they need a hand, snap at them when they do something stupid, and let them share their hunting stories as a way of continuing the best practices of business development. What feels really good is that I also have these conversations with my Alpha Female clients, and, as a result, other young Alphas are starting to duplicate my practices with their female colleagues. Authentic conversations in business are both contagious and addictive. I started my journey to becoming an old Alpha by having authentic conversations with proven Alpha Male leaders.

Beta Male

The Beta Male in business is the support player. He is the one who the Alpha hand picks to do the actual work that the Alpha Male sets up. He is the technician, the researcher, the planner, the strategist, and the manager. He is important because the Alpha Male needs someone to run the ball once he has thrown it. The Beta Male is one of two types: Either he loves the Alpha Male, but would never want to be him, or he wants to be an Alpha, but isn't sure how to do it. We refer to the latter type as a poser.

Alpha Males need Beta Males around to help do the work. We often call these guys our crew, and they play an important part in ensuring our success. Most Betas are either entertained or shocked by the Alpha Male. We are outspoken, and they are often reserved. We love to be the focus of attention; they prefer to be behind the scenes. We like conflict; they like everyone to get along. We have strong opinions that sometimes blind us, and they can see from everyone's point of view.

Although Alphas think that they are the whole show, in business it takes both types (Alpha and Beta) to get work done. In baseball, the pitcher is only as good as the catcher. The same is true in business. My friend Chad is a Beta Male. He is a taskmaster, he's organized, and he likes things to be done perfectly. He and I had a shared interest in a technology company, and he used to tease me because I got to go out for lunches and dinners with prospects while he sat in a small office overseeing the development of the actual programming products we were building. He and I would argue over when things would go to market; I wanted them ready as soon as a client was ready, while he wanted everything tested and retested to death before we sold it. He and I spent a lot of time arguing over schedules. One particular day, after much razzing from Chad about me playing around with clients over golf and supper while he was working, I invited him to join me for a day. I called it the "take a geek to work day." At 7AM, we met with the mayor and economic developer of the city as well as various service providers. Chad watched me put the connections together, making sure that everyone at the table had a sound, beneficial deal for themselves, and he saw the economic developer hand me their internal report on what they wanted to buy. We then had a lunch meeting before presenting to the city's IT department. Chad watched me lay out the strategy for a table full of Alpha Males and encourage them to let the city guy rant, as I knew he would. But I also knew we would finalize the deal with city council by week's end. Then we all headed over to City Hall where the IT manager—a Beta Male trying to be an Alpha Male—decided to take a shot at one of the service providers at the table. Chad watched this meeting of seven men quickly deteriorate into a pissing contest of dominance, which ended with me packing up my stuff and walking out of the meeting disgusted with everyone. That was a $3.6 million deal that totally went bust. As we drove back to the office, Chad said to me, "Sorry for anything I ever said about your job. I wouldn't do that for anything in the world." He seemed a bit shell-shocked, but for me it was just another day at the office.

The IT manager I referred to is the most dangerous type of man in business. This poser knows that he is weak and has decided that he can get control if he is devious and if he suppresses anyone weaker than him. Most women think that Alpha Males are the dangerous ones, but in reality the Beta Male is much more likely to make a woman's life hell in business. Alpha Males are looking for deals—as long as you don't get in the way you are relatively safe. The Beta Male, however, is much more malicious. He is a bully to anyone he perceives as weaker than him. He looks to dominate because he hates being dominated, which he normally experiences around Alpha Males. He will try to tell you what to do, unfairly judge your abilities, and undermine you to coworkers. The manager was a Beta Male in charge of the city's IT department. He was a weak man all around, but because we needed his approval for the deal to go through, he had a false sense of power and decided that he would try to leverage it against us, which didn't work out in his favor. He blew a deal for his city that we later installed in a competing city, and his mayor and staff knew that he was the one who corrupted the idea. He was a little man, and I noticed him dominating female staff on a regular basis. I always think of this type of Beta Male as the little boy who puts on his father's shoes and jacket and walks around the house like he is in charge. Then, when he hears his dad come home, he races to get everything back so that he doesn't get in trouble. The Beta Male can be a bully and a poser, but a smart woman can find ways to let the Alphas know that he is playing a role. Many of you readers who have dealt with a total idiot may have thought that it was an Alpha, but in all likelihood you had a Beta in daddy's clothing.

Alpha Female

The Alpha Female is an honored colleague in business. The major hiccup for her is that most Alpha Males think that women fake this and then wait for the first sign that they really aren't the driven professionals they claim to be. It has been my experience that Alpha Females are an extremely powerful force in business. They are goal oriented, they take full responsibility for outcome, they don't give up their power, they aren't overly aggressive unless the situation requires it, and they have everything they want. They know how to communicate effectively with all groups (Alpha Males, Beta Males, and Beta Females) to get the best out of them, and they are masters of powerful networks.

I often get asked if powerful women intimidate men. Definitely not! Beta Males are intimidated, but Alpha Males are impressed albeit a bit leery as to whether she is the real deal. To men, the Alpha Female in business is what the perfect man is to women in personal life. He's the guy who gives you flowers he grew and takes you to a restaurant he heard you and your friends talk about. He runs a bath for you after a long day and brings in a martini while you read the magazine he picked up for you. How many of you are thinking right now, "That would be nice, but that guy doesn't exist!" Well, they do exist, but as with Alpha Females, few can lay claim to knowing one. I think there would be a lot of Alpha Females out there, but they give up their power (which we will discuss later in the book) and men write them off as not being players.

I wanted to do some business with Royal Bank (a large financial institution in Canada) and asked my friend Karim, who is a broker, to introduce me to his manager so I could discuss a training program I had. As a man who provides a large female market with various products and services, I think that I'm aware of how to communicate with women to get my point across and build rapport. The manager, whose name was Lorraine, agreed to meet with me one morning. I decided that I would outline the program (process) and then discuss how we could work together (consensus) to achieve goals that would benefit everyone.

I walked in the branch and Karim showed me to Lorraine's office. She was closing a deal on the phone with one of her clients and waved us in. She finished the call, got up, shook my hand with intensity, and thanked me for coming to see her. When Karim left us, I prepared to follow my strategy. She looked me in the eye and said, "Mr. Flett, I'm sure you can appreciate in my business time is money. You have 10 seconds to tell me how you are going to make me money before I need you to leave so I can continue on with my day." I was shocked. This wasn't how this was supposed to go. I smiled and said, "I have a program that will allow you to train and track your roster of brokers in less time, making them and you more money." She asked me how much, I quoted her a price. She told me to pick some dates and send an invoice. She then smiled, shook my hand, and showed me to the door. If I wasn't already married, I would have proposed right on the spot. Having gotten to know Lorraine over the past few years, I know that she is the real deal. She loves the business, the people, and the art of deal making. She is someone I hold in high regard, and I'd do almost any deal with her seconds after she asks.

Strong men in business love working with strong women in business. When a woman is authentically strong and holds herself in high esteem, the gender issue starts to dissolve and she is considered an equal partner at the table. When I was starting in business my obstacle was age rather than gender. Guys would look at me and ask when the CEO was coming, not realizing that I was the CEO. But as I showed that I had the ability to put deals together with multiple profit models, my colleagues, who were most often 20 years older than me, forgot that I was the age of their kids and made a place for me at the board table.

If you love business and love setting and hitting goals, you are probably an Alpha Female. There are many men looking to do business with you, but you must not give up your power. If you do, you slide down the food chain from equal to below Beta, which is a bad spot to be in if you want to be in the deal. Men normally rank Alpha Females just below Beta Males because we assume you will sabotage yourself, but you can quickly move up the food chain if you don't play the role and give up your power to us. We respect strong women.

Beta Female

The Beta Female is, like her male counterpart, a support player. Charged with doing most of the things that need to be done, the Beta Female ensures that all the i's are dotted and t's crossed. The challenge with being a Beta Female is you start to melt into the background unless you have

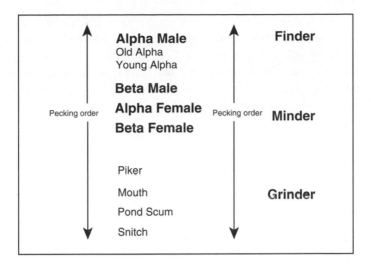

direct relations with an Alpha Male. Most Alpha Males take Beta Females for granted. Because Alphas focus so passionately on profitability, they direct most of their time on people who make money for them. We often see support workers as cost centers as compared to profit centers. Objectively we know that someone needs to collate reports, do research, answer phones, and plan travel. But subjectively, those things do not directly affect the bottom line even though they may support business development. Alphas feel like we can ride Beta Males much harder than Beta Females, and so we often prefer to work with them knowing that we can bend them but probably not break them. Women, on the other hand, are a challenging group of Betas because we are never sure if we might say something to bring them to tears. I know some people are rolling their eyes reading this, but how many of us haven't see a female coworker get upset by something at work?

A great way for Beta Females to get noticed is to interact with Alpha Males, ask questions, provide information directly, and be seen as a solution provider. I always say that the most important and powerful woman in any business is an Alpha Male's administrative assistant. She knows how he works, when he procrastinates, whom he likes and dislikes, and she is the keeper of his secrets. When he screws up and forgets something, he calls her. When he wants her to run interference against someone trying to see him, he lets her know. He will trust her and communicate with her like a confidant, which solidifies her role as being a very powerful and influential part of his team. Like Donald Trump, all big Alphas talk about their administrators. The presidential secretary decides who gets his time during the day, and in many businesses the administrative assistant knows more about a company and the various personalities than any other person in the company. She knows what the CEO is thinking and, through other assistants, what other individuals are doing in a company. The Beta Female is not to be overlooked as a force in business.

3

Getting Inside the Head of the Alpha Male

Men start assessing their peers as soon as they get an eyeful. I remember being the leader back in early elementary school, with all the kids looking to me at recess to decide what we were going to do. In my absence, my best friend would assume my role. Upon my return, he would resume his spot as Number 2. When I tell women this they laugh because it is so different from their experience. Men in school want to lead so that they aren't anyone else's bitch. Women want to lead in school (or be in the cool clique) because they want to have power over other people's opinions. In school, men are normally friends from when they first meet through most of their lives. A guy can be an asshole, and you will still give him the benefit of the doubt and hang out with him. Men are not judged by the company they keep. Women in school, on the other hand, can be best friends one day and enemies the next. They are so volatile that the strongest ones keep the weakest at bay for fear of confrontation.

From day one, men either lead or are led. It is as simple as that. I recall asking my dad how a team captain is chosen, as I was interested in the position on my fourth grade hockey team. He said, "If you want to be the leader, just assume leadership. The rest will follow. It is rare that someone will challenge you for your title if you act like it should naturally be yours." That advice has stuck with me throughout my life. There are natural leaders, people who enjoy being in charge, and then there is the majority who don't see the attraction of sticking their necks out.

Currency

Alpha Males assign themselves and everyone they come into contact with a place in their own imagined pecking order. We work hard to earn *currency*, which solidifies our position in society at a given time and allows us to strive for more. We have various ways of showcasing this currency to others in our social network. The currencies most important to the Alpha Male are: reputation, network of contacts, cars, vacations, homes, memberships, and of utmost importance, watches. These are things that we aspire to get and then, of course, to brag about. I always smile when I hear women talk about men who discuss the cars they drive or the things they buy. Ladies, you have no idea what bragging is until you are in a room with a bunch of Alpha Males. We brag like our lives depend on it. We are on good behavior when you are around, but when you aren't it is our secret shared pleasure. We are in a constant state of trying to be bigger while crushing each other. You know how women get together and start to talk negatively about their own body parts and then others jump in to talk about their problem parts? Well, men do the absolute opposite. One guy talks about his car, and the next talks about how his car has more options, goes faster, costs more, and so on. Rather than commiserating over our chubby bits, we instead puff up the ego and spend the afternoon in a pissing contest. I think that as Alphas grow through the ranks they develop different currencies that resonate with others in the same position. In the following sections I will talk about forms of currency that Alpha Males in various phases use as their show to others. I assign five stages to the Alpha Male and his position. Through his actions, you will know what level he is at and then how to better interact with him. From his homes and cars to his watches and memberships, he will brag about what he has and you will then know at what stage he is.

Stage 1—Freshman (<$50,000 a year)

This is a dangerous Alpha in that he is trying to get things going and will do anything it takes to get ahead. He drives as if there are no brakes, and he will crush anything in his way to get ahead and to set an example for others to stay out of his way. He hasn't much to show for performance so everything he does has to have immediate gains. This Alpha is almost entirely driven by a fear of not being worthy of being in business. He is quickly trying to figure things out before he gets rolled over by someone bigger, stronger, faster, or more experienced. His game in this stage is all about bluffing to get into the room.

Stage 2—Sophomore ($50,000–$80,000 a year)

The sophomore has the basic lay of the land when it comes to business. But by knowing how things work, he realizes how much work is required to be dedicated to being a contender. He probably is making some money, but with that money he is meeting people who are doing much better than him and it weighs on him daily. He urgently wants to get into a bigger game but starts locking into certain business positions (contacts, opportunities, contracts) to ensure he doesn't fall back. He is much like a rock climber who puts in an anchor before making the next climb. His fear isn't of not getting in the game (because he's in it), but rather of not being taken seriously. He is less focused on others at this point and more focused on doing things that are impressive compared to others. He is insecure with his abilities and particularly susceptible to criticism or perceived criticism. He has teeth if he needs them, but now understands the consequences of warring with other Alphas.

Stage 3—Junior ($80,000 $200,000 a year)

The junior knows the lay of the land, knows how things work, and has had a basic level of success. He knows how the game is played, understands the hierarchy, and knows which horses to hitch his wagon to. He knows that he needs to move from a sprinter mindset, which is to get business accolades as quickly as possible to a marathon mindset, which is basically doing the steps over and over again in cadence. He knows where he is on the ladder (middle) and is driven forward by all the people behind him. In the two previous phases he is focused on getting a place at the table and now he is trying to control who gets a place at the table. He knows that revenues talk and being able to pull the trigger all the time is the number one goal. He is now focused on connecting with other marathoners and making money together. He can taste the feeling of being a business leader and carefully watches himself to avoid missteps. He becomes more elitist, and people need to earn their time with him unless they are above him on the pecking order. He will attack if he feels someone is undermining him. If you are an earner and he sees strength in your alliance, he will connect, but if you are a boat anchor or easily give up your power, he will never consider you an equal.

Stage 4—Senior ($200,000–$500,000 a year)

The senior has been at the game for a while. He automatically makes money because he can pull the trigger regularly, has people bringing him deals constantly, and has garnered the respect of the market. He is more concerned with wasting time than wasting money and is at a spot where he can start to enjoy the work that he has created and what comes with it. Those in the lower stages all look up to him, and many bring him business as a buy in to do business with him. He is cautious about who he does business with because he doesn't want the fuss of having to clean up their messes. He is discerning with the work he does and believes that everyone needs to know how successful he has become through his vision and dedication. He is less dangerous to those below him, as long as they don't cost him money. If someone wastes his time or money however, they will feel his full wrath as he now has power to leverage in the market to make their lives very, very difficult. He is getting into a position of financial insulation, meaning that he would have to do a very bad deed (sleep with his secretary, get involved in a contracting scandal, etc.) to feel any financial repercussions. He will be a great running partner with you if you are established or if you can make him money by doing your business professionally.

Stage 5—Graduate (>$100,000 a month)

This is the old Alpha Male. He has been there, done that, gotten the T-shirt and sold a million of them. He is Mufasa from the Lion King. He takes pride in supporting other Alphas as long as they are worthy of his time. They must share the same interests as him and do business the way he wants it done or they simply don't get access. He starts to give back more at this stage and does so for appreciation of the market that built him rather than aesthetics. He makes money automatically and from a variety of sources. He enjoys hunting, but equally enjoys watching others hunt and being able to comment. He is the wise man of business. You can do a lot of things to screw up with a graduate, including costing him money, but if you respect him and try harder he will let it go. You get attacked or deep-sixed if you don't show him respect or don't honor him for his support of your initiatives. He can be your greatest champion and get you into deals, or he can basically destroy you with a few words to important people. The graduate is benevolent and can be your best supporter if you prove yourself worthy through your actions and loyalty to him.

There are a variety of signs, props, and activities Alpha Males use depending on what stage they are at. By understanding this information and observing, you can better engage with them and make your connection positive and selfishly beneficial.

Forms of Currency

Reputation

Reputation is an Alpha's strongest currency and the one he will fight hardest to protect. The trouble we run into with reputation is that because we brag about how great we are, we often overstate our abilities to trump someone else. Then we quickly need to learn how to do something so we don't look like an idiot. A young Alpha looks to align with bigger Alphas to learn how things get done and get credit for being involved in projects. A man is taught by his father (if he is raised by an Alpha) that a man's word is his bond. He must do whatever he can to keep his word at all time. This becomes a problem when we say we can do something and then it doesn't work out. I remember my dad telling me that reputation is like a bank account. When you promise something and deliver, your reputation goes up. When you promise something and don't deliver, the reputation goes down. If you build a strong enough reputation, you have all kinds of freedom. If you bankrupt your reputation, you are absolutely worthless. In a sense, Alpha Males are governed by the same rules as the mafia. I reference the mafia throughout this book because Alpha Males have co-opted them as a model for running a business. Have you ever wondered why men quote *The Godfather* all the time? Most of us love it. We learn how to be influence peddlers through modeling what we see on the big screen or television. I can always tell an Alpha Male by his love—not like—of mafia movies. It is not coincidence that we call the process of closing a deal "pulling the trigger." In these movies, as in life, when a man gives his word that something will happen, it isn't a suggestion, it is a fact. When he says it will get done, consider it done. The Godfather didn't say, "I will try to make this happen." He said, "Consider it done." Alphas want to develop a reputation for a variety of things, the most important of which are the ability to get a deal done (pull the trigger), the ability to make a lot of money, being the best in their industry, taking orders from no one, being a ringer, and being a guy who protects his own interests.

I have lost money in deals in order to keep my word. When I promise something, I always deliver—not because I always want to, but because I need to keep my word and grow my reputation. I am constantly looking for ways to improve my reputation. In 2003 I decided to go on a speaking tour and was warned by experts that this was impossible without a book. I then told those in my circle of influence (COI) that I was going to go on tour and I set a date. As I started to promote dates, things started off slow and I got worried, so I put on the afterburners and beat my prospecting list like a rented mule. I booked 46 cities in 73 days and was then told by my critics that this was an impossible pace to keep. I left home on May 10, 2003, and completed my tour. It was hell in a lot of ways, but I had made a decision, promoted my decision, and failure was absolutely not an option. At times when I wanted to quit and go home (I was on the road for the full time), I considered how it would make me look and I kept on. Exhausted when I returned home in July, I had kept my word and silenced my critics, all while increasing my reputation as a person who does things that people say can't be done. An important thing for women to remember is that the

Table 3.1   Various stages of the Alpha Male reputation

FRESHMAN	Relatively unknown by the market, and he tries to get his name everywhere it can be put.
SOPHOMORE	Some acknowledgement by a handful of professionals. Not known outside of his main markets.
JUNIOR	Well established in his main markets and in some secondary markets. He has built a name for himself and is getting recognition from smaller sector groups (chambers of commerce, industry associations, etc.)
SENIOR	Well known in his markets as well as a general knowledge of him by the market as a whole. Is seen in the media, and when his name is spoken, most people have an idea of who he is or at least have heard the name.
GRADUATE	Is the big dog of his market and is known by the mass market. Frequently covered in the media and acknowledged regularly by primary associations for his contributions. Think of recipients of "Man of the Year" awards, honorary doctorates from universities, and so on.

Alpha works on, develops, and guards his reputation fiercely. When men attack each other or deep-six women, it is most likely a reputation issue. For men, reputation and ego are tightly connected. If either takes a hit, we go all in and fight to get it back. I have seen women get deep-sixed for a simple comment that caused a man embarrassment. Within days, every man who witnessed it flooded the tubes and torpedoed her career. We will talk more about the deep-six, how it happens, and how to avoid it, later on in the book.

Network of Contacts

Another key currency in business is the network that we have at our disposal. Men and women build networks differently. Men look at people solely on business value first. I don't need to like a guy to do business with him. I need to know that he can deliver on what he promises (reputation) and that he can make me money. Then I start to collect people. I do this methodically by first writing down what I want my network to look like over a specific period of time. I decide on the type of people I want before I know who they are. I might write down that I want a corporate attorney in Los Angeles, a tax accountant in New York, a publisher in London, and a wireless provider in Calgary. Then I start to sift through my network for potential contacts in these areas. Undoubtedly, as I do this I get additional contacts that I wasn't prospecting for, but those are just more for the roster.

There is nothing an Alpha Male loves more than leveraging his connections to a client or colleague as a show of market strength. If I have a client who is looking to move into London to do business and is unsure of visa issues, I have two ways to support them. The first is to suggest that they connect with the consulate in London and find out the process. This is not the most impressive advice in that it is common sense and I'm adding very little value. The second, which I much prefer, is to say to the client, "Call Sid Lowey in London. I'll give you his direct number. He's a friend of mine, and he does this all the time for my clients. He can streamline and speed up the process for you. Tell him you are a friend of mine and he'll manage your account directly. Keep me in the loop, and let me know how it goes." In the first example, I'm like anyone else giving basic advice. In the second, I'm leveraging my network of people to make my clients' lives easier so they can make more money.

I'm constantly adding and dropping people in my network. New contacts with reputations go in; those who haven't delivered get dropped. It isn't personal, it's business. I'm looking to meet with and do business with the very best of the best wherever I go. People don't get into my network because they ask. They get into it because I believe they can deliver on what they promise and will make me look good in the process.

The other advantage to a network is that most Alphas are compulsive name-droppers. They use people's first names and wait for someone to ask who they are so they can drop the last name and the connection. Here's an example: A guy I was having cigars with in New York City a few months ago said, "I was working with my friend Ted in Atlanta on his cable company. We were getting some new programming underway and looking at the strategic plan for the next eight quarters." Of course, I was sizing him up and trying to see what type of network he had, so I ask the question, "Is it a local cable station, or are they big?" He replied, "Oh, sorry. It's Ted Turner. He owns CNN." He knows that by starting the story the way he did someone will ask about the company and he can name drop.

Many posers use their network as leverage, but really don't have access. I know guys who collect business cards, put them in their contact management system, and consider them a contact. The difference in my mind is the access that those people have. I hand out about 10,000 business cards a year, but would guess that only 150 people have my cell phone number. I would assume that many people have me in their contact system, but few can get me without going through the office. A network is only as good as the access that accompanies it.

Cars

The car is the Alpha Male's first big chance to showcase his earning capacity in business. This is more applicable to the young Alpha. Older Alphas may select a family-type car that is more appropriate, but undoubtedly he will have a toy to drive on the weekends. Cars are not only empowering to men, because we can feel our success each time we drive them, but we also get ridiculed about them if our car isn't up to par. I used to go to a program put on by my friend Michelle Pottle entitled Y.A.M. (Yoga Anonymous for Men—Yoga for men who don't do yoga). There would be 10 of us in the class, and at the time I drove a Jeep Wrangler. It had nice tires, and I'd have the doors and roof off in the summer. My friends who drove Audis, Humvees, and Porsches would stand outside the studio as I pulled up beside them and watch me park. Then they would get in their cars and move them to be away from my car. These were my friends! They would ride me before, during, and after the class as to why I would

Table 3.2   Various stages of the Alpha Male network of contacts

FRESHMAN	Knows people he went to school with, personal contacts, and limited business connections. He hungrily tries to add people to his database, and will add almost anyone that he gets a business card from.
SOPHOMORE	Is more discerning with his contacts. Tries to build contacts that build his business. Works rooms well and is good at acknowledging people he met before. He isn't great, but it also is apparent he has networked before.
JUNIOR	Has built a strong network of people who know people. He leverages his network to meet people that they know. He is clear about whom he needs in his network and makes it a priority to make these connections.
SENIOR	This is a master network builder. He has connections everywhere, and there is no one that he can't get to through his own personal network. He has people of strong reputation in all industries, and information is just a call away. He is tough to go to lunch with because he knows everyone.
GRADUATE	This is the senior statesman. He knows everyone worth knowing. People want to know him, be known to know him, and try to leverage their relationship with him to get things. Having a connection with him is currency many people use to their own advantage. His call gets through to anyone, and they are happy he called.

drive a Jeep when I owned a successful company. They would ask me if it came with complimentary duct tape, if I got a discount on my insurance because they would assume I was poor, and so on.

I was car shopping with my wife, Jacqui (she didn't like the Jeep either because it was high off the ground and hard to get in with a skirt). I found a BMW 5 series that had been converted to an M5 (the performance model of the BMW 5 series). I bought the car and started to notice things immediately: (1) I began to like valet parking (it's always disheartening when the valet can't get your Jeep to start), and (2) my friends weren't so fond of their cars now (as mine was now the nicest). I had jumped from the bottom of the car pecking order to the top. Now I was the one giving out the gears on the others' cars. I made tongue-in-cheek offers to co-sign a loan if they wanted to upgrade their wheels. I told them that I had considered buying a model like theirs, but didn't want people to think I was having financial difficulties. We use our cars as a flag to the business world that we have arrived and can buy the big toys. We slam American brands if we buy European. We slam lower models by the same manufacturer. If we drive the same model, we argue over options. To men, the car represents how they want the world to see them. Driving the Jeep, I was showcasing a small-town guy who hadn't let the money go to his head. Now the Beemer tells people that I like to travel in style.

Some of the cars that men most appreciate are Mercedes, BMW, Lexus, Porsche, Audi (higher series), Jaguar, Dodge Viper, and Range Rover. It is important to remember that the cheaper versions of these lines don't impress anyone, and men who drive them are considered posers.

Vacations

Young Alpha Males complain about taking vacations. They think that it wastes time and costs money rather than making money. I remember when Jacqui and I were going away for a weekend, and I told clients that I was going on a training course for the week and then hid my cell phone in a pair of socks in my bag so Jacqui thought I wasn't bringing it. I was terrified that clients would see my going on vacation as not being serious about

Table 3.3   Various stages of the Alpha Male automobile

FRESHMAN	Mud car. Normally the same one he drove in university. It is either cheap or cheap and shitty. If it is the latter, he hides where he parks it and, when necessary, rents something if someone is traveling with him.
SOPHOMORE	Normally a new mud car. A new Toyota, a new Mazda. Something that looks like it is new but isn't impressive.
JUNIOR	A higher-end car, normally used. A BMW, Mercedes, Lexus, Land Rover, or if new, some of the cheaper classes of these lines (i.e., 3 series BMW, Land Rover LR1)
SENIOR	High-end new car. $150K Porsche, $300K European convertible. Something that screams wealth.
GRADUATE	This is where it gets weird and somewhat tough to qualify, so you have to use other indicators. They either have a car like the senior, or they have a family automobile and a hobby car ('60 Chevy pickup, classic MG convertible, old school Corvette). Sam Walton drove a 30-year-old pickup.

business, so I lied. Now I realize that big Alphas need vacation to sharpen the saw. I like to vacation a few months a year and normally go to Miami or somewhere hot. Simply vacationing, however, isn't good enough when competing with other Alphas. We need to measure: length of vacation, class of flight, number of stars of the hotel, restaurants that you are eating at, activities, and a variety of other factors. We have a set of rebuttals for any comment a guy makes about his vacation. If a guy tells me he is going on vacation for two weeks, I ask, "Why so short?" If he says he is going to Jamaica, I ask him if Europe was too expensive. We give gears left, right, and center to each other. I have a buddy who goes to Cancun every year. He stays for a month and rents a villa. Another friend of ours goes there as well and bought a villa last time he was down. He kept it from our other friend until he said he was going down again, and then the one with the villa said, "Would you like to use my house while you are down there?" Total hit to the first guy! He graciously declined, but I know it ate him up inside. As soon as I heard that I thought to myself, "I need to buy a house in Miami!"

Jacqui and I recently traveled around Italy, and when female clients/colleagues ask me about it they always want to know about the sites that I saw. My male counterparts' first question is whom I flew with, and second where I stayed. This way they can calculate how much I spent on the vacation. I think women do this too, but more subtly; they ask where Jacqui shopped in Florence. As soon as I say Christian Dior, they smile, knowing that it's expensive. Only the Alpha Male can deconstruct what is supposed to be a restful and enjoyable trip and assess every angle to determine how it will make him look and where it will place him on the pecking order.

Homes

The Alpha Male loves his home, and it is the one place of solitude where he can recharge his batteries. I think that homes fall into two categories: a place where you entertain or a place where you retreat and keep private. I fall into the latter, while most of my colleagues are examples of the first. A couple of my friends have what most would consider mansions. They have 6,000 square feet and up. They have home theatres (rooms, not television packages), gourmet kitchens, and pools that look like they are out of an architecture magazine. They have bedrooms that no one uses, bathrooms only for guests, and bar areas accompanied by pool tables. I like to visit these people, and I wonder how much of their space is for them and how

Table 3.4   **Various stages of the Alpha Male vacation**

FRESHMAN	If he takes vacation (rare that they do), it will be a week somewhere warm and cheap, and he'll lie that he went somewhere better for longer.
SOPHOMORE	An all-inclusive trip for two weeks somewhere hot. (Old Alphas refer to these as mud spas.)
JUNIOR	Europe or a well-known resort somewhere tropical for two weeks.
SENIOR	High-end Europe, the Orient, or somewhere reclusive for two to four weeks a couple of times a year.
GRADUATE	Again, the graduate is tough. He might go to a small ski hill, but he will own the house there. He might fish on a quiet river, but take a helicopter to get there.

much is for show. In Vancouver's Yaletown (the old warehouse district), trendy lofts demand top dollar. They average $600–$1,000 per square foot and overlook the harbor of Vancouver and Granville Island, a trendy artisan shopping area and food market.

Anyone with a home here is total show. A colleague of mine who is an up-and-coming broker has a penthouse overlooking the harbor here. He drives an M5, has a home that would blow your socks off, but he doesn't have any furniture. Yes, I said it. He doesn't have any furniture. His car payment is $1,500 a month, and his mortgage is $7,300 a month. He rakes big money into his practices, but much of that goes toward entertaining clients. He is asset rich, cash poor, and doesn't have money for furniture. I have seen his place because I know him well, but he doesn't have any extra cash right now to outfit it, and it isn't a place that you fill with Ikea.

My mentor Alvin had a great place just outside of Vancouver. It had a game room, a deck larger than most of the apartments I lived in during college, and a collection of arcade games he bought for his kids. It was a great place to visit and I have never cooked on a better stove. I would guess the appliance was $10,000 alone. Simply beautiful. It didn't hurt that Alvin worked for Intel; the house was wired up like you have never seen. It was a technology paradise. I loved visiting his place and accepted any offer to do so.

I'm at the other end of the scale; although I have a nice car, my house is much more modest than these. It has all the toys, like the flat-screen televisions, antique scotch cabinets, and too many humidors, but for me my home is a very private place. I can count on one hand the number of colleagues I've had at my house, and I've never had a client in my home. For me, my home is a place where I step out of my role in the world and charge up my batteries. I learned this from my dad, who would come home, lock the doors, turn off the phone, and rest. I have thought about buying the big house and, in recent years, had the opportunity to do so, but for me the show doesn't happen there. Being to different houses I have noticed that the ladies in our lives check out the kitchens, the carpets, and the walk-in closets. All I care about is the television and the electronics. That shows me how the guy honors himself. I can't tell one carpet from the next, but I can spot a high-end sound system before I take my shoes off.

Alpha Males use their house as a club. They don't want everyone there as it drives the value of the invitation down. They will bring people there as a sign of trust and intimacy by showing where they lay their head. When you are in their home, treat it like a church, because to them it is their shrine to who they are. If you get the invitation from an Alpha Male to come over to his house, consider yourself in good standing. If you don't get an invite, but neither does anyone else, don't take it personally; it is simply his place of solitude from the world.

Memberships

Alpha Males love to be part of clubs—the more exclusive the better. There are clubs in various cities that traditionally have been what I would call the

Table 3.5   Various stages of the Alpha Male residence

FRESHMAN	Either lives at the family home, with a roommate, or with a girlfriend in a cheap place that doubles as his home office.
SOPHOMORE	A conservative apartment in a reasonable neighborhood. Probably no roommate, but may have a sweetie sharing the rent.
JUNIOR	Either a really nice rented place or a reasonable place that he owns.
SENIOR	A money place. He either owns it or pays high rent. It is in an impressive area and is made for entertaining. In most likelihood he owns it, and it is all about square footage. He might also have an apartment rented in another city.
GRADUATE	The big family house (think Kennedy compound) as well as a vacation property and an apartment in the city. Might have real estate interests in foreign countries as well.

"blue hair ball," where old guys with old money would sit around talking about their money and the only women allowed in the hallowed halls were service staff. Fortunately these groups are changing. Not because of a change of heart, but because their membership numbers have dropped. I'm still somewhat hesitant about these clubs, as I wonder if they are moving into the new paradigm or if they are just playing the role. Time will tell.

My club is a cigar club. It is located in Vancouver just minutes from False Creek, has a limited amount of lockers available for club members, and has its own smoking lounge. The front part of the business is a store with beautiful humidors and other smoking apparatuses and two full walls of exceptional Cuban, Honduran, and Dominican cigars. Just to the left of the front door is a lounge for members and their guests. You don't apply for a membership; you are invited when a spot comes open. If you aren't a member or with a member, the room isn't available. My friend Ted Loo, a well-known fitness professional on the West Coast, introduced me to the club. I was previously at one in Yaletown, but was feeling the average age was a bit too old for me. I was hanging on there because that is where my mentor Alvin and I spent a majority of our Friday afternoons before he passed. Ted took me to his club and introduced me to the owner, David. Through business endorsement (which we will discuss later), Ted had David give up one of his own personal lockers for me. I now bring clients there for business meetings, celebrations, or to make introductions between people I think will do great business together. I love when someone comes in and asks for me and then one of the wonderful hosts brings them to my section. They say membership has its privileges, and that is definitely the case for City Cigar in Vancouver.

Men use memberships to educate each other on their pecking order in society as a whole. There are clubs in Vancouver that are rumored to have $35,000 annual membership fees. Others focus on sport (yacht clubs or tennis clubs). The interesting thing here is that the more expensive the club, the bigger fish you find there. Again, much like the house or boat, I think it is better to have friends at these clubs then to join the club yourself. Your friend can take you for drinks, you can meet people, and you pick up the tab and save yourself about $34,900 in dues each year.

These clubs try to act selective by having a member or members nominate you. Then they take your application to a committee and decide if you are in. The bullshit part of this is no one really gets rejected. They aren't turning your money away unless you are the mob, a criminal, or if someone on the membership personally doesn't like you.

In my cigar club you don't have to pay a membership; you don't have to go through panel. If you are a stand-up person (reputation), you can get a locker when one is available. What I like about it is you have billionaire members and you have young professionals cutting their teeth in business. Clubs are important to the Alpha Male, but I think the type of club they join says a lot about what type of Alpha they are. Are they with a club that supports integrity, or are they with a club that just honors the financial ability? There are clubs that have tens of thousands of dollars in membership fees charged to each member each year and are basically a place to talk shop or to show off your membership card. In others, they take an active interest in building a community both internally with the members and externally with the city. A clear way to see what type of club it is would be to look at the requirements to be a member. You will be shocked by how many only have a financial requirement and a rule that three members have to vouch for you.

Watches

Okay, I'm about to indulge myself in one of my favorite topics and one that you can start using as soon as you read this section. Alpha Males love their watches. It is the one piece of jewelery that we can use to show that we have arrived. Let me paint a picture so you fully understand how important watches are to us. Have you ever noticed how when women get together they check out each other's shoes and purses? Then, when they are sitting together and one gets up, the rest catch a quick glimpse at her butt. They

Table 3.6   Various stages of the Alpha Male memberships

FRESHMAN	Hockey team, chicken wing eating team.
SOPHOMORE	Young Republicans, junior chamber of commerce, industry association
JUNIOR	Alumni association, cultural association, sometimes a church group, cigar clubs, some junior city clubs, golf clubs (initiation around $5,000)
SENIOR	Car owners club, club for professionals at a certain level (CFOs, CEOs, Senior VPs), investment clubs, city clubs (Union Club, Chicago Club, Vancouver Club, Terminal City Club, etc.), golf clubs (initiation around $20,000+), also major ski resorts (yearly membership)
GRADUATE	Horatio Alger Association

are doing this to assign pecking order in their own minds. Another way they do this is through engagement rings. Dior trumps Coach, Blahnik trumps Jimmy Choo, and so on. Well, in the Alpha Male world it is all about watches. When a man sits down with other men, he quickly scans wrists to see what other men are wearing. It immediately establishes the pecking order. I see a Timex, and I think mud. I see a designer watch, like Hugo Boss, Tommy Hilfiger, Armani, and I think wannabe player. I see a Tag Heuer, Oris, Omega, or Tissot, I think he's on his way but hasn't made it yet. I see a Rolex, and I think he wants to be his Dad. I see Patek Philippe, Breitling, or Cartier, and I think this guy plays big. Anyone who drops north of $7,000 on a watch is rolling big bank. The first thing I look at with any guy I meet is his watch. I'd like to say that I'm embarrassed by having a watch collection in excess of $70,000, but I'm not. And I'm just getting started. I have everything from Tag to Breitling and from vintage to new chronographs. With my crew of Alpha Males, the first time I wear a new watch they spot it before we are close enough to talk. I suggest to young guys I work with that with their first big paycheck they invest in a watch they don't think they can afford. I remember spending $2,000 on my first Tag Heuer and was second-guessing it. Jacqui encouraged me to get it, and the next day bigger Alphas started to treat me differently, but we never talked about the watch. My watches are not only my pride, but also a tool I use in business. If I'm working with smaller colleagues, I wear the Tag, or the Seiko Sportura. When dealing with the big boys, I break out the Breitling Super Avenger or a vintage watch. The only thing better than having an exceptional model is having a model that no one else can get their hands on.

Table 3.7   **Various stages of the Alpha Male watches**

FRESHMAN	Seiko, Timex, Casio, designer watches (Gucci, Coach)
SOPHOMORE	Tissot, higher-end Seiko, Sector
JUNIOR	Tag Heuer, Omega, Mont Blanc
SENIOR	Rolex, Breitling, IWC
GRADUATE	Vintage Omega, Rolex, Breitling, and so on (things you can't get in stores, collector's pieces). That said, the true Big Dog Alpha Male doesn't need to wear a watch. The world will find him if they need him. He is the master of time, not the other way around.

Most types of currency here are gender locked between men. Women also have their indicators to see how their colleagues are doing (i.e., purses, shoes, and of course the color, clarity, cut and carat of her engagement ring). I don't care what type of house, car, watch, memberships, or vacations that my female clients and colleagues have. I often have women asking me if I can tell what kind of watch they are wearing. In most cases I can't because it doesn't matter to me. I'm not comparing myself with them in that way. What I do care about is their integrity with their word (reputation) and their influence (network). If they have both of these, we are going to do some business. I think that is the benefit women have with men that they don't even know. We are not looking to set up a pecking order with you. We will never compete to be the bigger man with you. With other men we are on a dimmer switch. There are varying degrees of where each guy sits in our network. With women, it is either on or off. We either will do business with you or we won't. It is more cut and dry, which benefits you if you are in the circle and plays against you if you aren't. When you can determine which phase the Alpha Male is in, you know how you can best partner, do business with, and engage in a professional relationship with him. The prior information gives you a basic litmus test to determine what the best way is to work with him. What follows are the details of doing business with the five levels:

Table 3.8 What women can expect in the Alpha Male stages

FRESHMAN	He is dangerous to you. He is more selfish than normal, and when things aren't going his way he will look for a way to deflect responsibility and blame someone. This guy is toxic, stay away.
SOPHOMORE	An Alpha in this stage has some breathing room to build business, but is careful with how he invests his time. If you want to work with him, look for markets you can enter strongly together. He will assume he will rush ahead of you, so keep up and look at pulling the trigger yourself. If he thinks he's carrying you, he'll cut you loose.
JUNIOR	He is focused on developing channels of business. He knows where he makes his money (niche markets) and looks to become the dominant force in those markets. If you have access to these markets, or something that makes him stand out in these markets, start there. You need to be very clear on what you want and what you are offering for him to take you seriously. You need to be able to pull the trigger.

(continued)

Table 3.8   (**Continued**)

SENIOR	He has more opportunity than time and looks for people who through their work can make him more money. If you are exceptional at what you do and he can take credit for your work, he will work with you and make you both rich. You need to be on point because there are a dozen people behind you trying to be his go-to person. If you can deliver, you will have a great relationship. He doesn't need you to hunt as much as to deliver work product.
GRADUATE	He wants to teach. He wants to give back, but only to the worthy. He knows his opinion matters, and he wants to feel honored. Everyone wants something from him, so instead ask him what you can do for him first. Make your relationship with him contingent on you bringing value.

4

Things That Drive Men in Business

Here is the big secret that every Alpha knows, but no one talks about. Having had candid conversations with various Alphas in my life, I know this one piece of information to be so powerful, that we do whatever we can to cover it up

There is not an Alpha Male in the western world that isn't completely driven by his insecurities. Once we start making money, we fear that one day it will stop. We put up big fronts about our abilities, which are almost always an exaggeration, and then we quickly try to backfill before anyone finds out. It's much like a cowboy town from the movies. Looks good head on, but we will do almost anything to keep you from looking behind. I can't remember a day since I was 15 (and started making money) that I didn't worry about how much money I made or didn't make, how it compared to other guys I knew, and my spot in the pecking order.

Now as an adult, I am obsessed with insecurity of keeping the ball rolling. Every day CEOs around the world get up and ask themselves a question, "is today the day they find out I don't know what I'm doing?" That's why we are so aggressive when we receive criticism or consider something someone says as criticism. We think you have "found us out" and then we go on the warpath to take you out from a credibility stand point to try to preserve our ego. Below are some of the contributing factors to our insecurities and how we huff and puff to bluff our way into the big leagues.

How We Measure Other Men in Business

Alphas basically use a three-step process to decide if we are going to do business together: visibility, credibility, and profitability. We can use this process with each other quite simply because men have an honor code with one another. An Alpha won't date a friend's ex. He won't speak ill of another Alpha's family. When we give our word to another Alpha, it is our bond. We don't break our promises with each other. There is a basic level of respect we have for one another. Because of this we use the three-step approach to manage business relationships with each other.

Visibility

In this first step we get on each other's radar screens and know the place that we occupy in the market. Think of two dogs briefly getting to know each other. If we can come to a mutual understanding of the potential benefit of finding out more about the other, we take it to the next level, credibility.

Credibility

Once two men know about each other, they then have to explore if each other is exceptional at what they do and if they are at the same level in regards to performance. Once each guy knows that the other can deliver (sometimes this happens through small transactions between each other), they will start to do business together at an accelerated rate. Aside from doing business together, they act as market indicators for each other. If they hear something is coming up, they immediately tell the men they are doing business with to see who can benefit from the information. They start peddling the information that they are able to acquire.

Profitability

The two Alphas start to make money together. They honor the relationship and are focused on not being the weakest link in the relationship.

Once they get the money pumping, they just keep it coming in. Alphas don't need to like each other. They only need to respect each other in order for a business relationship to form.

When We War with Each Other, the Average Grudge Has a Shelf Life of 12 Months

Men can have a down-and-out fight, rip each other apart, sometimes even have a dust up (fistfight), and not talk for 12 months. Then they will cross paths, have a beer, and start to do business again. It's like a reset button gets hit after 12 months. We let things die and start again.

We Support Men, Even When They Are Down.

This is one of the biggest differences between men and women. Men cycle each other up, and women cycle each other down. Men are constantly driving each other on to get bigger, better, and more profitable. We use a proverbial racing crop to hit each other to move ahead. If I talk about the deal I just did, I have a counterpart telling me about the bigger deal he is putting together and so on. We are constantly moving ahead and challenging each other to keep up. We honor success and sweep failure under the carpet.

Women do the exact opposite. When one talks about how bad her life is, the rest of her support group jumps in to talk about how their experience is worse. Recently I was in Detroit sitting with a group of women at a table. One woman says, "My husband is the laziest bastard in the world." Then the next chirps in, "Wrong, my husband is a lazy bastard that makes your husband look hard working!" Then a third cuts in, "Sorry ladies, but my husband has the championship belt from the laziest bastard Olympics."

Why do you do this? Why is it important to find collective experience in the negatives? Society supports women being tough on themselves, whereas society forces men to live a big life. Anyone else see a problem with this? I was in New York at a big bookseller looking at magazines. One women's magazine had the following titles on the cover:

- "How to lose that flabby bootie."
- "How to get him back after he dumps you."
- "How to find peace with friends who betray you."

Are you kidding me?? These are brutal and you are buying this magazine to see how to manage a shitty life. At the same time, on the cover of a men's magazine that I think may have been published by the same company, were some of these titles:

- "The new Bentley. How to get it and why you want it."
- "Success factors every man needs to know."
- "How to live your best life."

Is there any wonder why men feel like they have an advantage regarding success? Men have the honor code among them, and we will help each other if we see someone is down, even if we don't like them. Time and time again I have seen a guy take a major hit in life and all his buddies rally around to pick him up, and even guys who don't like him will pat him on the back and help him up. Men honor the U.S. Army Ranger code that no man gets left behind.

Women on the other hand are the polar opposite. When a woman takes a hit and is on the ground, women rally around to stomp on her. Women seem to feel that by crushing one more woman, they are one more person ahead in line. Look at Martha Stewart. She's the sweetheart of the working mother: a strong businesswoman, an accomplished host and homemaker, and the CEO of a global empire. When Martha took a hit for alleged insider trading, it was women leading the witch hunt, not the men. Women said she betrayed them. Give me a frigging break! She stumbled, and women were quick to jump on her back to make sure she went all the way down. When women stop attacking each other and start supporting each other, the tides will change.

We Are Valued by Society on How Much We Make

Men are judged by society by our ability to generate wealth. Many will argue that being a good citizen, a good father, a good husband, a good friend, as well as a lot of other characteristics are what men should be judged on. I agree, we *should* be judged by all these attributes, but at the end of the day every man is judging every other man on his ability to make money.

Society supports this by glorifying big moneymakers as global leaders. Warren Buffett, Donald Trump, Mark Cuban. These three men are extremely wealthy and self-made. They have been elevated to the level of leader because they have made enormous amounts of money. Does this make them good men? Not necessarily, but they are at the top of the pecking order in society.

Our society worships money and assets. Young boys are exposed to this economic adoration while watching music videos and professional athletes. They even begin to take part is asset valuing by teasing each other about the type of job their fathers have. Just as women are judged on looks, men are judged on their ability to earn. It isn't right, but it is a fact.

Because men are judged by this, we start looking for angles on how to make more money. We go to college to get a good job, and either we are a great student or, as in my case, a very poor student. If we are academically gifted, we try to get a job at a big corporation where we can climb our way up to the top. We'll often jump to higher paying positions so that we can make more and more money.

Those like me finish school and, because job prospects aren't banging down our door, have to create our own jobs by starting companies. Although this is the harder path of the two, it allows us to generate wealth exponentially faster than our colleagues who punch a time clock.

When I started Think Tank, I had just left the utility company where I was making good money but knew that I would never make the money I needed to be in the winners circle. So I left the company and never looked back.

All my male friends who were in shitty jobs laughed when I told them I was going out on my own. "You are an idiot!" "I would have killed for a job like that!" "I bet Jacqui is looking forward to supporting you!" "Let me know if you need to borrow some money for noodles!" This was the support I got from my friends. My friends!

The fear started to settle in. Maybe I should have stayed with the job; I could have a future there. Maybe I made a big mistake. But in the back of my mind I knew that I was either going to win big or lose big, and winning big was what it was all about. My need to be a big earner gave me the courage to leave the confines of the company and form Think Tank. But before I get ahead of myself, let me share a little secret. My biggest fear wasn't of failing. At age 26, my biggest fear was Jacqui having to support me if I fell on my face.

I knew that every man in my life would think I was the biggest loser in the world for not being able to support our household. The fear of plopping to the bottom of the food chain was far greater than any cold call I had to make. And I *hate* cold calls!

Now this is the nugget. If you get in the way of a man making his way to the winner's circle, he will take you out before you see it coming. This is one of the reasons we go at each other. If a guy gets in my way on my path to making money, I will take him out. I won't even think about it. He'll fall out of the sky and wonder what's happened. I have had male counterparts get in my way regarding business development, and I have carried a big proverbial stick to beat them out of my way. Some of the guys I spend time with share a saying, "You are either on the steamroller or you are under it." Which in common language is "You are either supporting me, or you are wasting my time." When men go to war, it is either over money or ego.

We Fall in Love with Our Titles

Men love their titles. CEO, president, chairman of the board—these are titles we hold in high regard and that distinguish us in our company and in the market. The title represents, among men, our value in society. The president is more important than the vice president, who is more important than a director, who is more important than a manager, who is more important than a supervisor, who is more important than an employee. The funny thing about business is, without the employee, the rest of the positions are irrelevant. If someone isn't doing the work, the company is valueless. Still, we love our titles.

I know friends who have left positions for new ones with a better title and less money. Yes, I know men who have left jobs at established companies where they were "director of communications" making about $100K per year to become a vice president of a startup for $80K per year. The title allows us to bluff people as to how much money we are making, especially if it isn't a number we are proud of yet. Being the CEO of your own company holds more weight than being a regional manager within a corporation. If we pull back the curtain, that CEO may be making less than half of the regional manager's salary, but the assumption is he is making more.

Of course, within each level there are distinctions to stretch the pecking order, including junior vice president, senior vice president, chief operations officer, chief financial officer, chief executive officer. Then we break it down even more: vice president of marketing—Canada, vice president of marketing—the Americas, vice president of marketing—global. As you can see, we are so in love with our titles, we happily smother ourselves with the weight of the infrastructure necessary for holding up all those egos. Aside from passively showcasing to everyone we know how much money we make, men need these titles for two reasons: (1) To know the chain of command and the levels of power, and (2) so that we have something to aspire toward.

If there were no titles, we could strive to make more money, but people might not know. With an advanced title, a man should be (but not always) making more money than people with lesser titles.

Most men won't admit to it, but we love titles. It seems, however, that when we get into the winner's circle the title just doesn't matter anymore. When I first started out, I couldn't wait to tell everyone that I was the CEO of Think Tank. Now, when people ask what I do, I tell them that I work for Think Tank. It seems we are only prepared to downplay our title when we realize it really doesn't matter. It seems like entrepreneurs are much quicker at getting past the title issue than our counterparts working within a corporation they don't control.

We Fear Women in the Workplace

Since the Clarence Thomas case brought sexual harassment into the limelight, men don't know how to act. For too many years, men took liberties with female staff, and now we as a sex are so concerned about doing something inappropriate that we walk on eggshells when women are around.

Now I'm generalizing, but due to the amount of lawsuits and the fear of getting a reputation as allowing a hostile work environment, we are not sure how to act. When men are joking around and a woman comes in the room, everything stops because we don't want to be accused of using poor humor, doing something to make female colleagues uncomfortable, being thought of as a predator, or being known as a sleazebag in the office.

When we are acting weird, it is because our default switch is now set to clam up when there is a situation that could be misconstrued. One day while working on this book, I was listening to the news where a very attractive female reporter had just finished her bit and was going to throw it to the weather guy. But he wasn't there, so another male host (part of a two-man, one-woman anchor team) said, "Babe, you can throw it over here."

My head immediately snapped up from my laptop to the television to see this 50-year-old guy's face turn red and hear him say, "I apologize, that was a stupid thing to say." He was stunned as though he had just been punched in the forehead. The other male host tried to bring up other news, and the female anchor said, "Throw it to me, hon." and giggled along with the woman who was called "babe."

I know what that guy was thinking because I was thinking the same thing: He's going to get fired! I could just picture all the female viewers writing in, and I changed the channel because it was just so uncomfortable to watch him squirm. He had crossed the line. I do not believe that he was trying to be derogatory. I don't believe that he was trying to come on to her. I think that he is familiar with her and, in his comfort, said something that was not appropriate. Men know that today a comment like that is a career killer. Imagine one word being enough to finish someone's career, but it could. Men do not know what is acceptable and what isn't in most areas with women, and because of this we are cautious. I think that women need to educate men on how they like to be engaged. I have female clients who have guys hit on them or make passes. If they shoot them down directly, the guy gets bruised and wants to stay as far away from her as possible (pretend his failure to convert never happened). Instead, I suggest they try something like this example.

(Situation: Woman meeting a guy that makes passes at her for a coffee).

Gary: "How's it going?"

Lisa: "I'm having a rough day. All these sleazebags keep on hitting on me and making me really uncomfortable. Why do guys think they are charming when they are really being offensive?"

(This is a preemptive strike and should be delivered before he has time to make a comment).

Gary: "That probably is uncomfortable. What do you say?"

(He is fishing to find out what her indicator is for inappropriate behavior.)

Lisa: "I don't do anything; I just look down at my paper and hope they will move onto business. Guys like that wonder why they are single. Women find overly forward men repulsive."

(She has just talked about how men look horribly when they do this, and his ego now gets the message that in order to not look like an idiot he should avoid advances. Like Pavlov's dog, if he does make an advance, even accidentally, and she immediately looks down at her paper, he will know he just screwed up. She is now in complete control.)

Men don't know when it is appropriate to shake hands, hug, or whatever, so we will normally try to err on the side of being conservative. If a guy steps out of line and you don't want to embarrass him, use a generality the next time you run into him and talk about something someone else did and how cheesy it was.

Our Egos Are What Make Us Successful and Are Also Our Achilles Heel

Men get teased all the time about having big egos, but I'm going to share a secret with you. Our powerful egos that propel us ahead in business are easily cracked. When we are not doing as well as we think we should be, we dig down deep and find ways to keep driving towards the goal. Our ego is what we build business for. My ego is what allowed me to find success in self-employment.

When I decided to leave the corporation and start my own business, I put my ego out on my sleeve. If I wasn't successful, not only would I be known by other men in my life as a horrible business builder, but I'd also be the town fool for leaving a great job to go bankrupt in my own business. My ego propelled me ahead. That first year, my ego took a lot of damage, but also worked overtime to keep my head in the game. Shortly after forming Think Tank, I decided to call the other consultants in town and have a little chat about how we could work together.

I was aware that I not only knew very little about how to run a consulting business, but also that there were hundreds of things I didn't even know I didn't know! I wanted to have a meeting with these other guys to explore working arrangements (this is something guys do all the time). I was hoping that they would throw me some work to cut my teeth on, but I wanted to make sure I didn't look needy or weak.

They ended up talking down to me and telling me that they would "toss me some scraps" that they didn't feel like doing. I told them to stick it and that I was going to take over the best of the work and throw *them* scraps! I walked out of that meeting trembling, half with anger and half with fear that I had just committed professional suicide. Those guys did me a great favor by backing me into a corner where failure was not an option I could swallow.

I pushed hard to prove them wrong, and I'm proud to say that I did. My ego that first year was on a roller coaster. With every success my ego strengthened, and with every miss (See? I can't even say failure!) my ego would crack ever so slightly. Think of it as a man's power center. If injured, it takes time to heal.

One of my first contracts was to work with a publishing company to rewrite their marketing plan. I had the client sign a contract for $1,500 to do the work (a tenth of what we charge now), and I basically floated home. I was so proud of myself, and I had proven that I could go into the market and get work on my own. I couldn't wait till Jacqui got home so

I could tell her what I had done. I was like a dog waiting patiently but excitedly for the rest of the family to come in.

When Jacqui arrived I was sitting at the kitchen table with a big grin on my face and I had the retainer on the fridge. I was on Cloud Nine. I told Jacqui that I had got a whopping contract, and she shared in my excitement. She said to me, "Oh my god. Congratulations! You're like a real consultant."

Direct hit . . . boom! Picture an ice rink cracking. My ego had taken the full blow of her comment. I felt like she thought I had been pretending to be a consultant, that I had been playing the role of a consultant, but not seriously. Of course, now I can objectively look back and know what Jacqui meant, but at the time it took all the wind out of my sails. I said to her, "What do you mean . . . like a real consultant?"

She said, "Oh you know, I mean you set your mind to it and you have done it. I knew you would." I couldn't get past the comment. It's funny. As I write this, it is like I can feel that spot on my ego that still has the scar from her comment. A man's ego is not in his mind, as some would argue, rather it sits right behind his heart. I know this because that's where we feel the joy during good times and the pain when we fall. That was back in 1998.

When Jacqui graduated law school in 2004, I said to her shortly after, "Congratulations! It's like you are a real lawyer!" She looked at me and said, "Geez, will you get over it already?" That's how strong of an effect our egos have on us and how much damage they can take from an innocent comment. I love Jacqui. Imagine what would have happened if a female colleague had done that to me—deep-six for sure!

We Look to Cut Out Rather Than Fit In

Men often joke with each other about how women get their wagons in a circle and ensure that everyone is being included. Women are brought up to be inclusive and not to leave anyone behind. I think this might be hardwired into women.

Men, on the other hand, are pushed from day one to be special at something so as not to be a drone. Watch men engage with each other. We sit facing a little bit away from each other, and chat about what we are good at, what we have achieved, what we plan to achieve, and how great we are.

When women get together their body language is engaged. They either spend their time speaking nicely of each other or self-deprecating to keep one of the women in the group from feeling bad. Men call this "henning." Think of hens in a hen house. While the rooster is out on the stump by himself pissing everyone off, the hens are clustered up inside quietly clucking.

Another great place to observe this is in team sports. I've watched women in a team setting, and the most important part of the experience is the team winning. Men are very focused on winning, but we are equally focused on being the best at something. On every hockey team I've been on someone is the fastest skater, the hardest hitter, the hardest shot, the best defenseman, the best fighter, the best passer and it goes on and on. We each look for something that makes us special among our peers, even as we work together for team victory.

Women look to fit into the group, and men look to carve out of the group. We may still consider ourselves part of the group, but we really are looking for a position that shows we are outside and above the group. In business, we have positions just like in sports. I am part of a hunting pack, a group of professionals that are in complimentary services and that enter markets collectively, and in my hunting pack there is a set-up guy (gets the deal moving), the planner (develops the strategies), the position guy (gets us aligned with the right people), the risk manager (plays devil's advocate and protects our behinds), and the closer (a ringer who is brought in to get the client to sign the deal). We all know that if we each do what we do best, we are all going to benefit. We all are operating at the top of our game because we don't want to be the weak link and don't want to lose the title that we have carved out.

We Want to Take the Lead on Everything, but Don't Necessarily Want to Do the Work

How many times have you sat on a board with male counterparts who are excited to put their name forward to manage a project and then immediately after the meeting begin to recruit people to work with them to get the project done? At the end of the day we are successful if we have adequately delegated absolutely everything we can on the project and just watch over it. We do this to hedge our bets on the project. If we are successful, we can take full credit. If we fail, we have someone to sacrifice. This is a skill we learn from other men and model the behavior. As long as you keep taking on our work, there is absolutely no motivation for us to change.

I should add that we have perfected the model of leading committees. We offer to chair committees, and that makes us look like we are passionate about the project, but in reality it allows us to assign work rather than have it assigned to us. We then choose our team and give each person a task to do.

"Cheryl, you take care of meetings. Barb, you're in charge of meeting space and refreshments. Tabitha, you can manage the invitation list. Stephanie, you look into entertainment. Margaret, you look into funding for us."

We are so interested in not doing any work that we tell you to check with us if you have a problem, rather then us checking in with you periodically. If we don't hear from you, everything must be fine. Once we have assigned all the tasks, we have insulated ourselves from the outcome. If it is successful, we take full responsibility. If it fails, our only responsibility is we assumed our team members could do their jobs. Good for us; bad for you.

We Attack from Underwater When It Isn't Seen

The deep six is the Alpha Male's preferred weapon when it comes to taking another professional out of the equation. We like to use the deep six because it is effective, it comes without warning, it can't be traced back to us, and it totally neutralizes the person. It is so powerful that it can actually follow someone from career to career, and many recipients of the deep six don't even know about it. Let me share with you what it is, why we use it, and how we use it.

When we are embarrassed, criticized, undermined, plotted against, bad mouthed, or on the receiving end of any other activity we find offensive, we attack. When a coworker causes the failure of a project, fails to take responsibility, or is more of a hindrance than a help, we attack. When someone isn't able to deliver, whines, or is otherwise obnoxious, we attack.

When we attack, we use the deep six as our tool of choice. The deep six is the polar opposite of a business endorsement. Rather than put our name on someone else to endorse him, we make it very clear that the person does not have our endorsement. In essence, we blacklist him.

When a man deep-sixes a woman, he doesn't show any emotion, he doesn't recruit the support of others, and he doesn't do it in front of the target. He waits for the perfect time and then launches his passive campaign to discredit and undermine the person.

Here are some examples of the deep six in action:

Example 1

Rick: "What do you think of asking Gillian to come to the meeting?"

Me: "I'm not sure that Gillian would be my first choice."

Example 2

Allan: "Do you think Mary has partner potential?"

Me: "I think that all depends on what type of reputation we are looking to build."

Example 3

John: "Betty really got emotional in that meeting. That was uncomfortable."

Me: "I think all professionals need to learn how to be professional at all times."

Many may not see anything directly damaging in my comments. But to other men they are discreet ways of suggesting that the woman in question needs to be marginalized. The most powerful element in this type of attack is if the women ever gets wind of it and confronts the attacker, he can readily defend his position. Here's an example:

If I'm really going to deep-six a woman, I do it in a directed and swift way. Let's say that a woman embarrasses me in a business setting. I then get ready to take her out by calling her credibility into question. I go to an Alpha Male that I know and say something like this:

Me: "Do you know Christi?"

Fellow Alpha: "Yeah, she's in the business development practice with you, isn't she?"

Me: "She sure is. She is great, she is focused, and she is bringing in a lot of her own accounts. I think she brings a certain level of professionalism into the company. She wouldn't be my first choice to manage my client, but she is great."

Right there, I have just dropped a massive bomb on Christi's credibility with this Alpha Male. I then proceed to continue this discussion with every Alpha Male I know and who respects me. All of a sudden Christi feels like she is walking in glue and things are getting difficult for her, but she is unsure why. There is a chance that she will somehow hear what I said and come gunning for me. I'm prepared for that. I have a Plan B for total frontal attack by an angry woman. Here's what would happen:

Christi: "I heard that you said that I was focused, bringing in lots of accounts, bring a certain level of professionalism, but that you wouldn't choose me to manage your accounts. What's wrong with me? Why don't you think I'm good enough to manage your accounts?"

I know that Christi has a small part of her that wants to believe that this is a misunderstanding. She wants to believe that we can get past this and get back to working together. I know that she is emotionally charged, so I'm going to give her an out and create doubt in her mind. My reply:

Me: "Christi, first let me tell you that this is catching me completely off guard (at this point I'm smiling inside). Let me blunt. Can you handle blunt, Christi? I said everything that you just brought to me, but you have taken it out of context. I think you are great, bringing in business, and an asset. I will not, however, dump my client load on you. That's what men do here. I would rather give my clients for babysitting to someone who can't build, so that you can continue to do what you do best—bring in work. I'm not attacking you, I'm supporting you."

I can recognize that at this point some people won't buy it, but I have seen this done enough to realize that, regardless of the outcome, people will see her overreacting (if done in public and the rest of the men will deep six here) or she will be frustrated and on edge if it is just the two of us. Regardless, that dog won't hunt, and she has been fatally damaged.

I am not openly attacking her; I am merely withdrawing support of her, which sends a clear message to every other man. In the future, she will accidentally be omitted from team e-mails, her agenda won't show up in time, and the man, or men, who is deep-sixing her will look for creative ways to undermine her credibility further.

The most common ways to achieve this are by giving her work she won't be able to accomplish, sending her to meetings unprepared, and most important encouraging behaviors and actions that will sabotage her reputation in business. Men set traps for women and then walk away and let them hang themselves.

Many women who have been deep-sixed don't know what's happened until they realize that they are outside the professional circle at work. Female lawyers may watch men with less seniority make partner before them. Those in the financial sector may notice they are training their superiors. In other business settings, women may start to notice that they are constantly playing catch up on information that everyone else seems to have.

In groups that I speak to, many don't appreciate the power of the deep six. Let me give you a female example to think about. I'm 6'6" and 300 pounds. Let's pretend that I start working at a firm that employs a lot of women. One woman, who is respected by the group of women, makes the following comment in the women's bathroom:

Lisa: "The new guy Chris seems really great. He is already bringing in great files, which I'm really enjoying. He seems really polite, and offered to grab me a coffee when he went to Starbucks. I think he will be a really good professional addition to the firm. I wouldn't go to the basement alone with him, but I think he's a nice guy ..."

If you heard that from a fellow female worker, how interested would you be in accompanying me to the basement alone? Not many, right? You wouldn't know exactly why, but for some reason you would know that this wouldn't be a good decision. The same happens when a man hears you have been deep-sixed. He doesn't need to know why, but he knows to stay away.

The only way to avoid being deep-sixed is to gain power great enough that you become immune to its effects. You want to be in a position where individuals wouldn't even consider withholding information from you, where they will offer you partnership rather than lose you and your files, and where your colleagues and managers realize that you are an asset who cannot easily be replaced. This is done by doing one simple thing: becoming an earner for your company. If you can bring in deals, you become an asset rather than a liability and have in many ways insulated yourself from a deep six.

We Hate Criticism and Will Attack If You Call Our Reputation into Question

I have talked about our egos and how they drive us. Women who criticize men directly attack our egos, and this is something we refuse to bear. This is one of the quickest ways a woman can get deep-sixed, not only by the man she is criticizing, but also by every man in earshot.

Deep down most men are strong on the outside but soft on the inside, and we struggle with a fear of being exposed as a fraud by our peers. When we are criticized that fear starts to get realized, and we must neutralize the threat as fast as possible. That explains why the guy you criticized takes a run at you, but why all the other guys? Because we are afraid that you might criticize us next, and if we get rid of you we don't have to worry about you calling us on things.

A great piece of advice to consider is that you don't have to make anyone wrong in order to be right. Criticism is a judgment, and judgments get people into trouble, especially when they are voiced and even more so when they are voiced in front of a group. I'm not saying you have to sit there and take it, to be small and unseen, or to go along with something that is in conflict with your beliefs. The best advice I can give you is that criticism in the workplace rarely comes out in your favor. Women often ask how they can give constructive criticism to Alpha Males they work with so that they don't take exception to it. That's like me asking how can you tell a woman her butt looks big in a pair of pants without hurting her feelings.

If you are a boss of an Alpha Male, you can address a situation without making him wrong. Let's say that your Alpha blows a business presentation.

FIRST OPTION (resulting in a sabotage, deep six, or guy quitting)

If you said, "Rick, that didn't go well at all. You need to slow down and speak more clearly. As well, you need to remember what I told you about covering all the benefits of working with us." He will simply sit there and hear you out and then start looking for another job behind your back while launching a deep six attack at you. You have made him feel like your bitch by demeaning him (you may not have intended to, but that's how he will be feeling), and he now needs to abandon the situation.

Another way to approach this (Remember, you don't need to make him wrong to be right) would be to talk about this situation:

SECOND OPTION (getting what you want without tromping on his ego)

"Rick, I don't believe our clients understand what we are trying to deliver. I think it might be beneficial for us to slow down to make sure they aren't getting lost. Then we should decide what the key points are and hit it home until they get it into their heads. Then we can pull the trigger and move ahead. What are your thoughts about this?"

Here you have shifted some of the attention onto the client and asked him to work with you on a solution. Remember, men are programmed that when women identify a problem, they feel they have to fix it. So, let's let him fix it within your constraints.

If it is a boss or a colleague at an equal level, the simple advice is not to give advice, feedback, or criticism. Even if he says he wants it, he doesn't. No one can criticize him more than he does himself. He is his own harshest critic, and you will feed his insecurity by agreeing with his critique. He can't control his inner critic, but he can definitely go after his external critics. Men are sensitive to how they are talked to by women. Men give each other gears all the time so we disqualify any comments from men. But women, on the other hand, often speak their minds and this cuts deep. Men hear things very different than women say things. Here are some examples of what you might say and what the Alpha hears (all of these have the potential of getting you deep-sixed):

Table 4.1   Common communication problems with Alpha Males

WHAT YOU SAY	WHAT ALPHA HEARS
"I wish that meeting would have finished on time."	"You suck at running meetings."
"I'm surprised that client didn't come in."	"You can't pull the trigger effectively."
"I'd like a raise because I've been here a year."	"I should get money because I've stuck it out, not because I'm worth more this year."
"Why can't this team just get along?"	"You are really poor at managing people."
"You should go talk to Ben."	"You don't know how to do your job, manage your people, or control situations, so I need to point them out for you."
"I'd like to help you on something."	"You suck and need someone to pull your head out of your ass."
"Your wife must be a strong woman."	"You are a piece of shit who is lucky to have a woman."
"I think we need to pay more attention to the clients."	"You are asleep at the wheel and sinking this ship."
"You are setting unrealistic expectations."	"You are completely screwed in the head."

When women think they are being helpful with their comments, what they don't realize is they are shooting themselves in the feet. That whole 360-degree feedback thing was developed by a woman or a Beta Male. Alphas don't care about your feedback because we assume we are smarter than everyone we know. Give comments (criticism) at your own peril.

We Either Want to Be Exactly Like Our Fathers or the Complete Opposite

Men who have their fathers in their lives look to them as role models. As we grow up, the magic of our fathers either intensifies or diminishes. Our father is the first authority figure that we experience and is at the top of our pecking order for most of our young lives. When we hit our late teens and start to come to the realization that we have control over our lives, we either start to admire our fathers or are disgusted by them. This is important for women to understand, as it gives a unique insight into how men are wired.

I grew up in a house where my father was the dominating force. You did not mess with him, you did not disagree with him, and you definitely did not cross him. My dad and I had some disagreements, and I didn't talk with him for about a year when I was in college. During that time, I got my ear pierced, grew 2 inches taller than him, and was really starting to fill out. On top of that, I was bouncing at a nightclub and had an ego to match.

After we patched things up, I went for a visit. I was preparing for battle. I was ready to take a run at the Big Dog and find out if I could switch spots in the pecking order. When I saw him, his eyes went right to my pierced ear. I said to him, "nice, eh?" looking to antagonize him. He said, "It's not something I would do, but if it works for you, good." I was taken back. I was expecting the ridicule, teasing, and verbal nudging that I grew up with, but none of it was there.

I think that my dad saw me as a man for the first time and decided that his work was done. There was a graduation in our relationship that day. We started our adult relationship, and I was able to look back on some of the decisions that my dad made in my life and realized something important: He was doing the best he could with the information he had.

I put away a lot of my issues around him and held him in higher regard than I had before. I started to work hard at being a man that he would be proud to have in his family, and I started to model myself after his work ethic, approach to business, and how he conducted himself. Some of my other brothers, who didn't have this experience with my dad for whatever reason, are complete opposites of him. They don't get excited about their work; it is a means to an end. For me, my work defined me for a lot of years and still does to an extent. This is something I share with my father.

If you are wondering why a guy acts the way he does, take advantage of any chance you might get to meet his father. You will see a slightly older version of him or the black to his white. Whether or not we admit it, we all live in the shadows of our fathers. Any guy who says that his father hasn't influenced him is lying; even if his father wasn't in his life, he was almost certainly influenced by his father's absence.

We Are More Focused on the Goal Than the Process

One of the most common frustrations felt between men and women is speed and focus. Women are experts at process: deciding what has to happen, who will do what, when it will get done, and all the characteristics required to successfully complete a task. Men have a strong ability to jump into the fire and shoot from the hip. We love to get deals going, position and strategize relationships, and close deals. Our strategy is shoot, ready, aim. Women check the winds, have a good look at the target, decide what tool to use, ensure that the right person is using the tool, support that person in using the tool, aim up the target with the tool, ensure that nothing is going to get in the way of the shot, prepare to shoot, double check that the shooter is ready, and then fire. You can see the difference between the two.

Women are more successful in business as a whole because they think out the process and do their homework. Men are not as successful as often, but when we are it takes us one tenth of the time to get there as our female counterparts. Women honor responsibility, while men honor risk. These two viewpoints are naturally at odds with each other. When men are rushing, all they are thinking is goal, goal, goal. Women see this and determine that men are shortsighted and lack attention to important details. Men watch women going over the details with a fine-tooth comb and think, "Wasting time, wasting time, wasting time (and money)."

The following illustrates this point. Two female colleagues and I sat down to discuss a client we were going after. I do business development, one of the ladies does sales, and the other does marketing. They started talking about all the things we know, all the things we need to find out, and all the things we have to prepare. I finally piped up and stated, "Just get us a meeting, and I'll close the client." They looked at me smirking (they know me well) and asked, "What are you going to say to them in the meeting?" I said, "I don't know, I'll figure it out in the meeting." We all had a laugh together because we've had the discussion before about the differences in approach between men and women, but it is true.

I have a lot of appreciation for these two women because they are masters of their areas of expertise, but it is ear-bleeding murder for me to have to sit and listen to all the details. I'm just not programmed that way. They, on the other hand, think that although I'm successful I'm cavalier in my approach, and it would make them feel better if they had more information before going into this meeting. I understand that their approach works for them, but to me it's a waste of time.

The only time men are interested in process is if it is absolutely necessary in order to hit our goal. When I'm going on a trip to the United States, I question colleagues who have traveled there to find out what is the best way to get from the airport to the downtown core, what their process was for developing their network, and other process information that can offer me a shortcut (read: advantage) to get to my goal. If I can't clearly see the advantage I'll get from hearing the process, I tune it out.

Think of how men watch sports. We watch Sports Desk or Sports-Center so that we can see every goal, touchdown, body check, and high-light of 30-plus games. We don't watch a hockey game to see how well people pass, how the lines change, how they warm up. We watch for that spectacular moment when one team shows its dominance over another by scoring that ultimate measurement: the hockey goal.

PART II
Female as a Saboteur

5

Bailing Water: Taking Things Personally

Have you ever...

1. Felt that you have been passed over for an opportunity?
2. Asked a client why you weren't chosen for a project?
3. Asked a colleague why you weren't selected for a team?
4. Felt left out of a business function?
5. Felt that you had a great relationship with a client, but they gave work to one of your competitors?
6. Felt that you have given support to someone else (client/colleague) but aren't feeling that they are supporting you back?

Women get a bad rap in business for being too emotional. "Don't take it personally, it's not about you. It's what's best for the business." Even though we hear these words, they still aren't easy to take. In a perfect model, business is apolitical, asexual, and objective. Unfortunately, humans mess things up by bringing our own issues to situations. Business is built on personal relationships, but individuals who aren't positively affected by the decisions that are made should not take those business decisions personally. This is easier said than done.

When decisions don't go my way, I have tried in my career to examine what I could have done differently, why the clients made a decision against what I considered to be best, and what I might have done that had a negative impact on the outcome. As soon as I get in this mindset, I stop and reset myself. Business is business. It isn't personal. Decisions made should reflect what is best for the business objective. This is a hard pill to swallow, but a necessary one. What I always try to do is to remove myself from the situation and look at the business side objectively. I ask myself these questions:

1. What are five potential reasons why I wasn't chosen for this project?
2. Were there any personalities that were in conflict in the decision-making process?
3. Was there political influence at power here?
4. If I was in their shoes, what would I decide?
5. What are some of the potential negative effects had I been successful?
6. What can I learn from this?

I generally find that by looking objectively I can see why things go the way they go. In the last year, our communications company was asked to bid on a proposal to work on a much-challenged area of Vancouver to conduct some research and build a revitalization plan for the area. This area is ridden with prostitution, drugs, homelessness, and a lack of business continuity. When I read the request for proposal (RFP), I smiled to myself. This project was made for us. We not only had success in doing similar work in other parts of the province, but we were experts in the area of development that was being requested. The RFP was issued over Christmas holidays, and although I usually don't work over the holidays I thought, "Don't look a gift horse in the mouth." I spent a few days developing our proposal and was very confident that the work had been cut out for us, but we would still have to go through a bidding process. I knew for a fact that no other company had the experience and the success that we had, and we were not only frontrunners, but really were the company the board was hoping to hire.

We submitted our proposal along with five other companies. Within a week, I wasn't surprised to hear that we had been short listed with one other company to do a presentation to the board. I arrived to do my presentation and heard that the other company had shown up late and had just started their 45-minute presentation minutes before we arrived.

Rather than getting upset, I smiled to myself and thought, "Rookie mistake. They showed up for the presentation late. Poor way to make an impression!" I sat back and read the paper as my fellow consulting firm did their shtick for the committee. My confidence was high before I got to the offices. You can imagine how confident I was after seeing my competition 40 minutes late for their presentation. As they left the boardroom, one of the board members rolled his eyes at me. As the other group passed me, I introduced myself and held out my hand. They said "Hi," and left without shaking my hand. I thought to myself, "Poor losers."

As I walked in, the chair of the committee informed me that he had to go because he was late for an appointment. He shook my hand and said, "Good luck." This didn't really faze me because he would only be leaving if he was confident with us and his fellow board members felt comfortable interviewing me. The remaining board members and I knew each other. I had done planning with this group, and we got along well.

The board member who took over for the chair began by saying, "Well, Chris, tell us about yourself." We all laughed, as we knew each other very well. They asked what I knew about their association with a smile, and I told them that I knew a lot about their group as I had done their strategic planning session, worked with their executive director in policy development, and had audited their business development plan. I left the meeting on a high. Deal done! They told me that they would notify the successful candidate by week's end.

That Friday, I called the executive director to find out the results and she informed me that the board had chosen the other company because they had a Cantonese-speaking consultant on their team. I remember driving back to the office in shock. This was totally impossible. I knew these people. They knew me. They knew we had done the exact same work with exceptional results. This was impossible. I took it very, very personally.

I spent the rest of the day in a haze. That night, upon waking, I considered the following things: What are some reasons why they hadn't have chosen us? Were their any personality influences? Were there any political influences? How would I have decided if I were in their shoes? I realized the company chosen was actually located in their area. They had existing alliances with many of the groups that would be involved. They probably knew things about the area I wouldn't know by not living there. And although they didn't have the experience that we had, they had a vested interest in the outcome. They would have to live with the project if it wasn't successful. The stakes were very high for them to succeed.

It would be hard for the association to promote internal trade in the area and bring in an external consulting group. They had to walk the walk to be authentic. In my approximation, they did what was best for the area and made a solid business decision. By taking time to put away my personal feelings and deconstruct the situation, I can see that the decision wasn't personal . . . it was just business.

Many of my female corporate clients tell me that Alpha Males in their lives often take credit for the work they do. Sitting on boards or teams, the Alphas will often say they'll do the work, but then leave it to the female participants, who they know will pick up the slack. Then when the project is done and successful, they take all the credit without giving any recognition to those who really did the work. What I tell my clients is hard to swallow but true: Men get promoted to their highest level of incompetence.

Women who work on projects for which male counterparts take the credit have an enormous value to those men. Those men don't forget that they didn't do the work. They realize that the women who helped them are the ones they need to keep near. My dad always said, "It is far better to be the kingmaker, than the king." This is true. The power lies in those who position others in places of prominence. You insulate yourself from any fire that might come, and at the end of the day you know how to do the work, he doesn't. This makes you very, very valuable.

Many of my clients say to me, "Yes I understand that, but he's using me." I contend that women have control over how others interact with them. Don't take responsibility for the outcome if someone else already has. If someone wants to make big claims on what they can achieve, make sure they have enough rope to hang.

The truth is men will often give women work to do that is way beyond their responsibilities. This can be a great opportunity for women looking to move up in business. Try to think of it as a chance to dig into something that you might not otherwise get to try.

It's as though you are working for a construction company where the manager is always drunk, sick, or away and you are responsible for doing his job. You could look at it and think, "I'm not getting paid enough to do this job." Or you could think, "I'm learning how to run a construction company even though I was only hired to be an assistant."

When the time comes to move on to a construction management job, you have excellent answers for your interview questions. When they ask questions about your experience, you can say, "I was hired by Company X to assist the manager, but due to workloads I was often required to cover the manager's responsibilities, including scheduling subcontractors, filing city documents, going over plans with the architects, managing the work-site, interacting with clients, bidding on contracts, overseeing payroll, and managing site budgets."

If you look at an incompetent boss, coworker, or colleague as an opportunity, you will excel in business rather than being frustrated by not being appreciated.

If, even after objective examination, you still seriously think that someone is out to get you, you need to take some precautions. I always tell clients that weak men try to dominate face to face; strong men attack and you'll never see it coming. If someone has it out for you and is trying to make your professional life hell, you have two options: Accept it or find a new opportunity that fits better.

I'm always a little bit cautious when I have clients who take things happening at work to heart and then feel that they are being excluded from key meetings, are not being given opportunities they deserve, and that they are getting blocked from advancement due to men climbing the ladder ahead of them.

There isn't a sane businessman out there who doesn't recognize that performers get whatever they want if they are making the company money. I work with several female lawyers who are looking to make partner in their respective firms. It seems that their male counterparts are much more likely to make partner than they are, and they are frustrated at being overlooked. They start to take the treatment personally.

They say to me, "I've been loyal to the firm. I work hard. I stay late. I am there whenever they ask me to be. My work is impeccable." I ask them, "What do you think the requirements are for being partner?"

They say, "You have to be a great lawyer who represents the firm well. You have to have a chosen field where you excel. You have to help build the firm. You have to have a long-term vested interest in the firm's success. You have to have influence in the community. Things like that."

I respond, "One thing sticks out in my head, not only in your ability to become partner, but also to take back control over your life as a lawyer. You said that building the firm is a prerequisite to becoming a partner. My guess is that the partners of your firm are bringing in more business than they can do. They are building the firm's value with new clients they are attracting through their reputation, community connections, and their reputation. Fair to say?"

The client will respond, "Yes, I think that is very fair to say."

Now it's time for the hard question, and it is received the same each time I ask it: "Are you bringing in more work than you can handle or are you servicing the clients who come in or are referred to you?"

The client will often have a sheepish smile on her face and say, "Mostly I do the work that I get. I'm not bringing in a lot for others."

Almost upon saying this, the client realizes that the glass ceiling isn't there to keep her down, but rather to separate the hunters from the grazers. In business, those who can hunt call the shots for those who wait to be fed.

By appreciating that it isn't a personal vendetta that a female lawyer has a 15-year call yet still isn't a partner, the individual can assess why partnership hasn't yet been offered. From a business stance, she simply isn't bringing in enough work to enforce the golden rule for herself. I'm not a lawyer, but in my estimation as a business developer if a lawyer, regardless of sex, is bringing in $750,000–$1 million worth of work, it is in the best interest of the partners to make him or her partner. If the existing partners don't offer partnership, the lawyer can simply leave and start a new firm. If you only bill enough money to cover your own salary and expenses, why would equity in the firm be offered?

Free enterprise is a brilliant system in that the quickest, the most forward thinking, and the most driven businesses and business people will take the top part of the market. Individuals who focus on taking things personally will be passed in the left lane by those who realize that business is just business.

6

Singing Sirens: Wearing Masks

Have you ever...

1. Brought cookies or baking to work for your colleagues?
2. Suggested someone take Vitamin C, Tylenol Cold, or other remedies for a nasty cold?
3. Walked a birthday card around to have colleagues sign it for someone's birthday?
4. Offered to organize an extracurricular business event?
5. Been overly dominant in a meeting to let men know they can't step on you?
6. Talked over male colleagues?
7. Cleared the table after your colleagues have eaten to make room for the meeting to continue?
8. Quietly sat and waited to be of service/value in a meeting?
9. Pretended you liked hockey/basketball/golf so that you have something to talk about with your male colleagues?
10. Gone to the pub for beers (and you don't like beer)?
11. Drank more than three alcoholic drinks at a corporate event?

12. Flirted heavily with a coworker or client?
13. Slept with someone in your industry?

When I bring up this behavior in seminars, I often see women looking down or getting mischievous looks on their faces. Women have been taught to play roles in order to achieve some type of control in personal and professional situations. Before coaching women in business full time, I spent years watching women in business settings and watching the adjustments they made depending on the situation. I'll explain the top five masks that women wear when the time comes to step out of authenticity and assume an anterior role. These masks may appear to engender powerful results, but in the long term they undermine the integrity and professional credibility of the women who use them.

Bitch

The Bitch is the one mask most men and women identify quickly. This mask leads the wearer to dominate the situation, create demanding scenarios, and let the world know that she will not be taken for granted or underestimated. She lets everyone know that there is both bark and bite to her words. She strides into meetings like Cruella De Ville and categorically demands both male and female counterparts know she is a force to be reckoned with. Male counterparts often refer to a woman in this mask as a Femi-Nazi, mad dyke, man hater, ball buster, or other crude slang names.

In my experience, the Bitch is often the most committed and passionate professional, but she's tired of being taken for granted or having a submissive position. She strives for complete control to ensure that she doesn't lose control.

One of my first female business mentors was a stereotypical Bitch. Let me tell you that she was never a Bitch with me, but I would watch the transformation when we would go into particular meetings. I recall sitting in her office in the downtown core and talking about development projects. She would have a huge smile on her face and would be excited about all the things we were building. Acting as counsel for those in development-type jobs is very exciting and educational. A person gets to see how projects go from vision to development, and you create very trusting and mutually beneficial relationships. I knew this individual very well and had been through good projects and bad projects with her. She was taken for granted in the city we worked, and she seemed to always be fighting an uphill battle for credibility.

One day in particular we met before a board meeting to go over a strategy we were trying to get a buy-in for. We came up with our game plan and were joking back and forth on our way to City Hall. When we walked into the front door, her persona shifted right in front of me. Her walk altered into a Darth Vader death march, and she entered the room with an unspoken force. She came across as being in a very bad mood. She responded to all inquiries with terse one-word answers.

When we presented our suggestions, she glared at everyone she had decided might speak a word against the idea. Sitting there, I thought that I might have said something to piss her off in the car and had instigated this bad mood. She hit comments against our idea with heavy force. She took turns taking runs at the opponents of our idea. The men in the room started gunning for her, but luckily time was running down and the chair suggested a vote. The vote was passed in our favor and the meeting was quickly adjourned. I followed her out of the hall, trying to keep up with the strident march.

As we got into her car, her persona returned to the way it was before the board meeting. Confused, I asked her what had made her so mad (and I was hoping she wouldn't say me). She said that she wasn't mad; she was serious and wanted everyone to know how seriously she was taking this project. Having spent a lot of time with this individual, I thought I could be blunt and stated, "You came off like a wicked witch in the meeting." She told me that men wouldn't take her seriously if she didn't approach them aggressively. They would walk all over her if she gave them an inch. She told me that a few of them were obviously gunning for her by the stupid questions they were asking to bait her. I sat there for a moment stunned. She and I had perceived the situation in two very different lights.

After a few minutes, I said to her, "They weren't gunning for you. They hadn't read their board packages and were looking for information to get up to speed so they knew what you were talking about without admitting that they hadn't done their pre-meeting work." She told me that I was wrong and that those men all had problems with strong women. This was the first time I realized how differently men and women saw the same business situation.

A week later we were heading back into another board meeting, and I said to her, "Would you consider adjusting your approach as an experiment? I think if you look at the men at the table and know that they haven't done the pre-work, yet they still want to have deciding power, you'll see their questions will have a different meaning to you. If your approach adjusts, I think we will get consensus much more quickly." She told me that she respected my view, but I was too young to understand business politics in a small town. I told her that I was prepared to put my money where my mouth was and forfeit my monthly retainer if I was wrong. She smiled and said that she was prepared to take my money.

On the trip to City Hall, I went through each of the Alpha men in the room and profiled them for her in my eyes and how I thought they needed to hear the information. She listened intently and asked a lot of questions. I suggested a course of action, which would be more in line with how she acted with me and would be closer to her authentic self. She smiled and said that she would be sorry to take my money and show me the truth, but thought that it would be a useful lesson for me. We entered the room, and she said good morning to everyone.

The male participants' demeanor toward her had drastically changed from the last meeting. They smiled at her, and they quickly got to their seats when they saw she was ready to start. She looked at me curiously and began to introduce our idea. She recounted what was in the board package and stated the benefits to everyone at the table and how it would be implemented. Upon completion of her presentation, one of the largest Alpha Males in the room held up his hand. Her persona changed to Bitch mode in preparation for what she thought would be an attack. She looked over at me as if to say, "I told you so!" The Alpha said, "I'd like to put forth a motion to approve this project before us." You could have knocked her over with a feather. She was assuming he was going to question her on the project, but instead he championed the idea and the board passed the idea unanimously.

The Bitch feeds directly into the Alpha Male's need for conflict. They will rarely go head-to-head with the Bitch, but they will begin undermining her authority with the crowd by keeping her out of the loop. The men in the group will ignore what she has to say, do things to frustrate her hoping to make her cry and show weakness, and forget to invite her to key meetings. Some will go as far as to set her up for a fall so that her credibility is damaged beyond repair. I've seen women who wear this mask excluded from activities because the Alphas say that she is too difficult to work with. Putting on the Bitch mask plays into the rules of the Alpha Male. They love conflict and someone looking to pick a fight. It is one of the quickest ways to get ostracized from the group.

You might wear the "Bitch" mask if you:

- Engage in verbal combat in the boardroom
- Think that a strong defense is a strong offense
- Feel it is important that nobody thinks you are a push over and want to prove it by making examples of other people
- Declare open war on individuals you think have wronged you
- Try to talk over people to be heard
- Use intimidation as part of your business strategy
- Unload on people whom you think are treating you unfairly

Geisha

The Geisha is the polar opposite of the Bitch. The Geisha sits by quietly and waits to be called into service by one of the men in her circle. She is quick to run for things that were forgotten, never speaks a word in opposition for fear of being rude, and looks for direction from others. The Geisha is the female version of the "Yes Man." Whatever is the will of others is her command.

When asked for her opinion, she will state the case for both sides and then say, "Gee, its tough to decide as both sides have their strengths . . . what do you think?" Indecision is better than the wrong decision for the Geisha. She arrives to meetings early, makes sure that everyone has a coffee cup and the copies of the materials that they need, and is quick to volunteer for everything that nobody else wants to do. She thinks that service will propel her to advancement, but her lack of decisive abilities stunts her upward movement. She is not a clutch player. She can't be counted on for the tough decisions.

Every company has its share of Geishas. They are often great workers and know what should be done differently, but by stating that they will be criticizing someone else's work, so they quietly sit back and hope that someone else will notice.

I have seen a lot of Geishas in business settings. Regardless of industry, they are at almost every boardroom session. They are the ones who make you wonder, "Why were they there?" I remember one Geisha in particular who sat on a steering committee with me. She would sit and watch everyone debate the issues. After every meeting I thought to myself that she was a waste of space on the board. When asked for her opinion, she would regurgitate what everyone else would say and then smile. She was like a secret stenographer of the board. She just repeated what everyone else said.

People would smile when she talked, knowing that she would carefully maneuver from any position and then try to focus the discussion on someone else's opinion. People would question in smaller groups why she was on the board. She offered absolutely nothing in the way of conversation. I remember on one occasion the chair saying to her, "We know what everyone else has said, now I want to know your thoughts." She sheepishly smiled and said she wanted more time to think about it. She had absolutely no credibility with any of the board members and was later asked to step down.

You might wear the Geisha mask if you:

- Know things should be changed, but are scared to say so
- Look at how to do as much as you can for others
- Sit by and wait to be called into service
- Will not offer an opinion on anything for fear of offending
- Spend most meetings quietly observing and offering nothing in regards to preference or suggestions
- Are insecure of what you bring to the table

Whore

The Whore is a mask that is either worn almost always or rarely. The Whore mask is the one women use when they attempt to use sexuality as a power over their male counterparts. This can be one of the most toxic masks a woman can use. The Whore role is often accompanied with sexy clothing, innuendos, colorful jokes, talking about sex lives, or taking liberties with male coworkers/colleagues.

Everyone has seen the whore mask at an office Christmas party, where the guilty party has had a few too many drinks and is a little more friendly than normal. Moments of indiscretion during a party or drinks with coworkers will paint a proverbial scarlet letter on the office door of the offender.

The rule for men is no more than three drinks within 24 hours during a business setting. Not to say that men don't break this rule, but those who are serious about having strong reputations and thus strong businesses will ensure that they are seen in the proper light at all times in business. When the Whore mask is put on, nothing will ever replace it. Professional reputation will be built in light of the personal reputation acquired at a time of weakness.

One example that pops into mind about the toxicity of the Whore mask happened to a colleague of mine. She was an exceptional executive director and often spoke at conferences regarding her ability to leverage assets others assumed impossible.

At a conference held in the United States, she bought into the Road Rules slogan—"What happens on the road stays on the road"—and acted extremely inappropriately in front of individuals who knew her on a professional level. She started off by getting drunk, sitting on the lap of another prominent manager, and telling him how much she was attracted to him. She did this in front of 12 other colleagues sitting at the same table in the pub. After this gentleman kindly maneuvered around her advancements, she went to the bar, picked up a stranger, and went up to her room with him.

The next night, after having another dose of liquid courage, she approached the gentleman with whom she spent the previous night and, after he blew her off, she picked up a friend of his and accompanied him upstairs.

Both of these situations were in full view and scrutiny of her new and existing colleagues. On the third night, she wore a bathing suit top and slacks to dinner. She was attempting to put forth a strong sexual prowess, but only achieved snickers and disgust from those who knew her. I wasn't at this conference, yet the managers that I saw in the following weeks were quick to recount their experiences in witnessing her activities and how she embarrassed not only herself, but also those in her delegation from the West Coast.

To say that her time in this market was short-lived would be generous. She had committed professional suicide, and after being released from her job she had little opportunity and was forced to leave the province. She went from the top of her game to the basement in a matter of three days. Sex does not equal professional respect.

Another example of sexuality overplayed was on the television series *The Apprentice*. The men and women were split into two teams to sell lemonade. The team that sold the most lemonade would win. The men tried to garner attention by putting big deals together. The women on the other hand tied their T-shirts up in the front and offered to sell lemonade and a kiss for $5. The women on the show were very attractive and they won this event, but Donald Trump and his advisors were noticeably disgusted by this course of action. It showed no talent, little thought, and an advancement of stereotypes of beautiful women in business.

If you are counting on sexuality to support your advancement plan in business, no matter how attractive you are, you will simply run out of resources and potentially be run out of town. Women who use the Whore mask disgust the women around them and are seen by men who work with them as very dangerous.

You might wear the Whore mask if you:

- Like the way cleavage gets you attention
- Enjoy the notice you get when you wear short skirts
- Think it's okay to let loose at company parties when everyone is drinking
- Use sexuality to get what you want in professional settings
- Use sexual innuendos to garner professional male attention
- Think that it is okay to tell off-color jokes in business settings
- Think that flirting is a tool you can use to get what you want

Man

The Man mask is the easiest for men to catch women wearing. Men constantly look to see if a woman is the real deal or to verify if she is playing the role. I would say that about 20 percent of the women I know in business at one time or another put on the Man mask. Women who talk about things that I ascertain they know nothing about have little credibility. Let me give you an example of a Man mask wearer from personal experience.

This woman was a colleague who does information services for small businesses. It was in the middle of the hockey playoffs, and she said to me, "The playoffs sure are exciting this year, aren't they?"

At this moment, I think to myself, "Is she looking for something to talk with me about, or does she really like hockey?" So I qualify her by saying, "Are you a hockey fan?"

She replies, "I'm a big fan. I love hockey. I watch it all the time." In the mind of the Alpha Male she has now either dug a big hole or is the real thing. I wanted to see if she was playing a role, which would sink her credibility with me, or if she was the real deal and I'd engage her with some conversation.

Me: "What do you think is the biggest thing that the Canucks have going for them?"

Her: "I think they have a really good team."

Me: "Who's your favorite player?"

Her: "I really like Mark Messier." *(Because I know that Messier plays for the Rangers, I ask the mask-confirming question.)*

Me: "Do you think he can take the Canucks to the Stanley Cup?"

Her: "I wouldn't be surprised."

Boom! Direct hit. She has just self-destructed in front of me, and the only way she is going to know is if after our discussion she finds out that Messier isn't a Canuck. At this point, I tune out the rest of our conversation.

Remember the old saying "Don't bullshit a bullshitter."

She just committed professional suicide with me. In order for her to have any credibility with me, she has a long, long road to walk just to get back to center.

There are a lot of backwards authors and advisors of women out there who think women need to learn how to play golf, go for drinks at the club, or talk hockey in order to get into the boys club. Nothing can be further from the truth.

The people who get invited into the game are the people who bring something to the table. If you aren't authentic, you can't be trusted. People who are trying to be authentic will look to partner with people who also value integrity and authenticity. Women don't have to become men in order to be successful. In fact, they should appreciate that they hold a lot of the skills that men attempt to learn.

Authenticity is the foundation of the new paradigm of business. Wearing the Man mask is dangerous because when women do this it becomes the subject of great conversation among men when women aren't in the room. We take great interest in women who think they have to be man-like in order to be a contender. Women who don the Man mask deep-six themselves with men in their network.

If you can't walk it, don't talk it. Guys will call each other on bullshit, but we won't call women on it. We just make a mental note and tune out everything else she has to say.

You might wear the Man mask if you:

- Talk about things you aren't interested in but you think men will want to talk about
- Talk about sports but don't watch them on television

- Try to get inside the boys club by taking part in stereotypical male activities
- Try to replicate your male counterparts in a way that feels unnatural to you

Mother

Of all the masks women may wear the Mother is the favorite. A Mother is the person who brings cookies to work, gives relationship advice, takes Tylenol to the person with a headache, and cleans up after everybody in the lunchroom. Mother remembers everyone's birthday, plans the company picnic, and makes excuses for people when they haven't done their best. When the crap work comes up, men look to the Mother to take care of it. The Mother is never taken seriously and is seen one day as a godsend and another as a waste of a salary. How much would she accomplish if she put the time into her job that she put into trying to take care of everybody?

Most women are predisposed to the Mother mask as they are naturally caregivers and concerned about the welfare of the group. I often help clients get over the necessity to mother professional contacts, including me.

One client and I were sitting outside having lunch this past spring and I said to her, "Gee, I'm cold." She quickly called over the server and asked for us to be moved inside. A few minutes later, I said, "I don't know what I did with my napkin." She got up and got me another one. I then said, "I'm thirsty. I wish the server would bring more water." She poured half of her glass into mine. I sat there and smiled at her.

She looked up and said, "Damn you! Are you testing me?" I smiled at her. This was the fourth session in a row where she automatically tried to fix whatever I brought up. The Mother is never seen as a serious businessperson because the Alpha assumes that her need to help everyone trumps her ability to be objective in a business setting.

There is a difference between being courteous and aware of the needs of others and trying to take care of everything for someone. It is appreciated but not respected by the Alpha Male. If I am with a male counterpart and he says, "I'm cold," I'd say, "You should have brought a jacket with you." If they say, "I wish that server would bring more water," I'd say, "Wave them over and get them to bring more." I won't do it for them for a couple of reasons:

1. I assume that adults can take care of themselves.

2. If I do it for them, I'm letting them know that I think they are incapable.
3. If they can't take care of themselves, I definitely don't want to do business with them.

You might wear the Mother mask if you:

- Are always keeping an eye on remedies you can share with people
- You have Kleenex on your desk just in case
- You make notes of your colleagues birthdays and the birthdays of their family
- You are in charge of planning surprise parties
- You think there is always a good reason to bring fresh baked goods to the office

The Consequences of Masks

There are unspoken consequences to mask wearing. Men rarely talk in mixed company about the masks, but we do when we are alone. We inventory the women we know professionally and assess which, if any, masks they wear. When we go through this inventory, we talk about the lack of authenticity and how women who play a role can't be trusted because you never know which mask is going to show up when you call a meeting. They aren't dependable, and we, as men, can't be sure what to expect from women who are playing the role.

We are worried that keeping company with a mask wearer will make us look bad—like we're not in control, we keep bad company, we endorse losers, or that we have caused or justify the mask that is being worn. I remember on one occasion having to send a female contractor home because her dress was inappropriate for the presentation that we were about to conduct.

In the world of the Alpha Male, women and people in general who play the role of something they aren't are a total waste of time and resources. When I see the mask come out in someone I know, I'm disappointed. When it is on someone I don't know, I make a conscious decision at that moment not to take him or her seriously. I want to deal with real people so I know where I'm at with them. If I have to guess, I don't want to play.

Masks are suitable for Halloween and theatre productions, not the boardroom.

7

Dead Calm: Putting Ideas in Question Form

Have you ever...

1. Tried to build consensus by taking one of your ideas and saying that everyone on your team came up with it?
2. Asked if something was a good idea, even though you know it is?
3. Had an idea shot down by someone who didn't know all the details?

Try this quick little quiz to see if you have ever given your power away by putting your great ideas into question format and had Alphas dismiss your great ideas:

What your idea was	How you brought it up
Moving into a new market to take advantage of an opportunity	"What does everyone think of opening an office in San Francisco?"
Bringing on additional staff to allow sales people more time to close deals	"Would it be a good idea to bring on support for the sales team?"

Going after a prime client of the competitor because you heard they were unhappy	"Do you think we could make a move to take their telephone client away?"
Cutting costs to make a department profitable in the short term until revenues come up	"Do you think the department could be more profitable if we made some cuts?"
If we get a hospitality suite we can attract new customers to the company	"Do you think if we got a hospital-ity suite we could attract new cus-tomers?"
You have proven data that there is a niche market that can be opened profitability.	"Is it worth exploring the Italian market in New York City? There might be some opportunities there."

This is one that is a sleeper for most women. They don't realize how often they offer ideas in the form of a question. Women are natural consensus builders and more likely than not are concerned and focused on getting buy-in from the group. This is strength in business. Yet, when women form ideas in questions men interpret it as them floating an idea and assume that they haven't really prepared for the meeting and will dismiss it.

Consider how you share your ideas. Instead of asking, "Do you think that the merger is a good idea?" adjust and say, "I think that the merger is a great idea because it will increase profitability, stabilize our market, and cut down on costs." The second example allows you to offer your opinion and back it up with the reasons for your viewpoint. Even if your colleagues don't agree with you, it shows that you have put the time into justifying your viewpoint. This will open up discussion and allow for increased conversation or internal affirmation of you and your firm's viewpoint.

Following are four suggestions on how to prepare and feel more at ease in offering ideas with integrity and confidence.

Do Your Research

When you have ideas that you want to put forward, the first step should be to rationalize why you are taking a stance on this topic. No one likes someone who is just throwing out ideas, unless it is in a brainstorming session. A quick way to lose credibility is to offer ideas that haven't been thought out.

A few weeks before federal elections in Canada I had dinner with a friend and I asked who she was thinking of supporting. She threw out the party's name, and when I asked why she had chosen them she said that she liked what they had to say. When I pressed her for more information, she dodged the question because she hadn't read any policy, but instead had listened to people she liked about how they were going to vote.

The best way to have credibility in any discussion is to share your well thought out ideas with passion and knowledge. People may not agree, but they will respect you for having the ability to be concise and strong in your beliefs.

Take a Chance

Sometimes you have to go back on what you originally thought when more information comes to light. We make decisions on experience that we have, and I have experienced situations where I was very passionate about one thing that later turned out to be wrong. There is nothing glorious about sitting on the fence waiting for the perfect moment to state an idea. Sometimes you have to assess the situation, develop an idea, and put it forward. You may be right or you may be wrong, but in the end you have been proactive with idea development and everyone will appreciate that.

Prepare for Creative Conflict

Every time you put an idea out there some will love it and some will hate it. That's just the way that it goes. In my experience, it is about a 50/50 proposition. When professionals disagree respectfully, often a higher-level solution results from the conflict. Don't avoid conflict; rather look at it as a tool for development.

At the end of the day agreement may not be achieved. The important part of offering your idea is to ensure that people heard what you said and that you heard their comments. Too many times in business, professionals focus on what they are going to say next, as opposed to actively listening to the other person when they talk. Seek first to understand and then to be understood. If you strong-arm adverse ideas by blocking out what they have to say, you are doing yourself a huge disservice.

Be Confident When You Are Sharing Your Ideas

Being meek will not offer you the opportunity to be heard. Remember that confidence is attractive, and if you are doing things right and bringing business to a new level, there will be some people who will disagree because in their minds change is not good.

Imagine if Christopher Columbus had said, "I'm wondering if anyone else has thought that the Earth might not be flat? Do you think that it could be round?" Instead, he said, "The Earth is round, and I'm going to set out to prove it. Who is going to join me?" He had as many critics as he did supporters, but at the end of the day he is remembered as a visionary and a confident explorer. To be successful, you have to paddle hard, get on the wave, and ride it.

Stranded: Making Excuses

Have you ever had something go sideways and shared with others why you think it went wrong? Have you felt that you owed someone an explanation for what happened? As soon as you offer an excuse you have basically put yourself at the will of whomever you are making the excuse to. It is now up to them to pass judgment on if your reason is worthy.

Men look at each other and roll their eyes when women break out into an excuse for something that has happened. Because we are goal driven, we don't care about what gets in the way of the goal. You either did something or you didn't. We don't care about why it didn't happen; we are interested in when it is going to happen and how you are going to make it happen. Let me give you "Chris's notes" on excuses.

No One Cares

When you give an excuse you see it as offering an explanation, which means you are discussing process, which we don't care about. Now it seems like you are content to waste more time by trying to explain why you weren't able to do something. Rather than spending time making excuses, look for a way to get it done and do it. Excuses are just another way to waste time.

Giving Up Your Power

When you make an excuse, you open up your actions to criticism. The excuse gets analyzed by everyone who hears it, and they determine if your reason for not getting something done is reasonable. This totally undermines your power as a professional because you are allowing others to make a judgment on your actions. It does not matter what they think. Let me use an example to illustrate the point.

Stacy was late for her board meeting due to an unforeseen family issue. She arrived to the board meeting 15 minutes late, and the chairperson had to rearrange the agenda to account for her tardiness. She is one of three women on a board of 15. This was her approach when she walked in:

"Hi everyone, sorry I'm late. My daughter was up sick last night, and her school doesn't let kids come to school if they aren't feeling well so I had to wrangle up childcare. By the time I caught a cab it was already 9AM. Sorry about that."

When Stacy presented this to the group, the women nodded their heads. They understood challenges involved in balancing family and professional lives. The men, on the other hand, were thinking:

- "Why are you wasting more time with that stupid explanation?"
- "I don't care. I don't care. I don't care. Just sit down so we can continue."
- "Don't trust Stacy with responsibility, she'll blow it if her kid gets sick!"
- "Why wouldn't you have childcare set up before you need it?"
- "Can we just get on with this?"
- "Pathetic."

Stacy has opened herself up to criticism on her ability, or lack there of, to manage her personal and professional lives. She thinks it has given them information to understand what her challenges were, but what she has really done is given them just enough information to make a judgment on her actions. Stacy has given her power up to the room.

This is what Stacy should have said to acknowledge that she didn't fulfill her team's expectations and at the same time kept her power: "I'd like to apologize for my tardiness. I appreciate being a part of this board, and I will take every possible measure to ensure this never happens again."

By approaching the situation in this way she is acknowledging that she didn't fulfill expectations and will take actions to avoid it being duplicated. Done! Nothing said about what happened, why it happened, and so on. None of it matters to the guys.

If there is a guy in the group who is looking to deep-six her, he will try to bait her into giving an excuse by asking, "What happened?" or "I hope that everything is alright." Her best response here is just to say it was a personal matter. This will stonewall him, and they can all get back on to business. Do not take the bait! You do not have to make excuses to anyone.

My wife, Jacqui, is a very powerful businesswoman, and I used to tease her about making excuses. I'd bait her to see if I could get excuses out of her, and she was extremely proficient in stonewalling me.

When she was in law school, she was working with a professor doing a research project around the United Nations. She wasn't feeling well one morning, and she told me that she was going to call in sick. I suggested that she not make an excuse to him, just to tell him when she would be in. She gave me a snarky look and said, "I don't make excuses!"

I smiled at her and said, "We'll see." Jacqui got her determined face on and picked up the phone.

She called the professor and said, "Good morning Dr. Jones, it's Jacqueline Flett, and I won't be coming in this morning." She stopped and looked at me. I have to admit I was a little bit shocked, and I was about to clap when she continued, "I haven't been feeling well all morning. Last night I started feeling sick, but thought by this morning I'd be feeling better but I'm not."

I started to smile and mouthed the words, "Excuse!" She glared at me and continued to give the professor more details on not feeling well. She went silent and said, "Tuesday at 11 AM," and hung up. When I asked her what he said, she said, "All he wanted to know was when I was coming in." I laughed and said to her, "Nice excuse." She shot back, "That wasn't an excuse; it was an explanation!"

Women are much better communicators than men and love to give details to add color to their stories. The problem here is women share ideas that are process-focused, not goal-focused. All Jacqui's professor wanted to know was when she was coming in (goal). As a general rule, when talking with women add the flavor, but give men the information in a goal-related format. This is what Jacqui could have said that would have shortened the conversation and been more appealing to the professor: "Hi Dr. Jones, I won't be coming in today, but I will be in Tuesday morning. Talk with you soon." That's all he wanted to know.

Looking for Approval

When you offer an excuse, what you are really looking for is approval of your situation. When you seek approval, you give up your power. Do not do this. It doesn't matter what others think. I know that is hard to hear and believe, but at the end of the day, if you are doing your best, that is all you can offer. It doesn't matter if they think your reason for not doing something was good or not. You either did something or you didn't.

If you did it, that's great. If you didn't, what are you going to do about it? Don't be the golden retriever that goes over for a pat on the head. You are a proud, powerful woman. Take on that role and act like it. You don't need anybody to justify your existence. Every time you want approval for your excuse, you are looking for that pat on the head, and every man knows it. You are putting yourself in a bitch (submissive) role to stronger men. Don't play that role.

9

Walking the Plank: Declaring Open War

Have you ever...

1. Gotten into a fight with a friend at work?
2. Felt wronged and decided to bring attention to the injustice publicly at work?
3. Spoken out against something someone did that you didn't agree with?
4. Told someone they were wrong in front of colleagues, bosses, or clients?

One of the most noticeable ways women and men are different in business is the way we go after each other. Women roll out the cannons, prepare the revenge plan and go to the mattresses (if you don't know this term, rent *The Godfather*).

Men, on the other hand, attack like sharks. You don't see it coming; you can't track it or know when to expect it. It just comes out of nowhere, and then afterwards you collect the remaining pieces. When we attack, we don't want anyone to see it or to be able to trace it back to us. Conversely, women walk up and stick the knife in the front and the back. Men just stand back, mouth agape in wonder. There are three things that men observe when they watch women go after a colleague in a professional setting. Here is one of my favorite examples:

I worked with two women at a job with a utility company right out of college. One's name was Debbie and the other was Beth. They were two peas in a pod. One was in the marketing department and the other was in the branding department. They were best friends. One would bring baloney, the other bread; one would bring salad, the other dressing. They would have lunch together every day and chat about life. One day I'm standing at the photocopier and Debbie comes up to me. She says, "You know Beth?" I replied, "Yes" (of course I knew her—they were attached at the hip every day). She then said, "Yeah, well Beth is a total whore. She slept with the photocopier guy!" I looked her in the eyes, picked up my photocopying and went back to my cubicle. Unbelievable. Who says something like that to a coworker, especially an Alpha Male? Later that day Beth came up to me and said, "You know Debbie? She is a horrible mother. She would come out partying with me on weekends and leave her kids with her mother. What a tramp!" It's funny. Debbie going out wasn't an issue until they had their falling out. These two professional women worked their way through the department slamming each other. What they are really doing is trying to build teams against one another.

I'd hear one of them say, "This is what happened, do you think I'm overreacting?" If the person said "No," then the gal would add this person to her team. If the person thought she was overreacting, she would say, "You don't know, you weren't there!" and move on, striking that person from the list of alliances. What they both succeeded in doing was letting every Alpha know never to trust them with anything for fear of them spilling their guts if they turn on you.

Following are some of the main things I've witnessed and that men talk about when women go at each other or even when they try to go after a guy.

Women Show Vindictiveness When Trust Is Breached

When women go after someone, they go after them full force: full steam ahead, emotional, taking things totally personally, and going for the jugular. Often they'll set themselves on fire to take out the person that they think wronged them. In the heat of their anger they forget this is almost a kamikaze approach. Women forget the environment they are in, and if they do remember, they just don't care. She becomes like a pit bull attacking.

Men refer to this as a cat fight, or the "hens pecking at each other." It is such a sad way for a woman to give up her power. This is almost always driven by what is considered a breach of trust between the woman and a coworker.

Undermine Trust in What Was Shared (Telling Secrets)

Once the attack has happened, the woman on the attack then goes around and looks for supporters for her actions. She starts with those who are most likely to be supportive of her position. Even though the men will nod their heads in agreement, they are thinking: "This chick is psycho!"

You'll hear her make comments like:

- "What was I supposed to do, he stole my idea!"
- "I'm not the one who started this! She threw the first punch!"
- "I reached my breaking point! What would you have done?"
- "I can't think of anyone who wouldn't have done the same!"
- "That's what he gets for getting in my way!"
- "I warned him that he was pushing me!"

After the attack, everyone tries to stay out of her way. It isn't because they fear her; rather, they don't want to have anything to do with her. Without knowing it, she has just excommunicated herself from the group. This will be something she will have a hard time overcoming, mostly because no one will tell her that she has passive aggressively been punted from the group.

Undermine Trust in What Was Shared (Telling Secrets)

This one is a killer. When a woman is scorned and she is ready to go for the throat, she starts spilling her guts on every secret she knows about that person. The gloves are off and discretion is out the window. Anything that was told in confidence is now fair game in trying to destroy the other's reputation.

The quickest way to undermine your integrity and give up your power is to declare open warfare on a coworker. You make a spectacle of yourself, you give everyone in the vicinity a good reason to get rid of you, and you show that you have absolutely no control over your emotions. If there is reason to attack, do so with discretion, but don't leave a trail, and don't let them see it coming.

10

Loose Lips Sink Ships: Not Keeping Secrets

Have you ever:

1. Given your word you would keep a secret but then shared it with someone you trust at work?
2. Known a work secret and told your spouse or another family member?
3. Talked about confidential things after you left a job?
4. Talked about the politics between two or more people at work?
5. Talked about an uncomfortable situation at work that you witnessed?
6. Shared a juicy bit of gossip you heard secondhand that was entertaining?
7. Ever shared gossip you heard about another company with coworkers or in your business environment?

Men assume that women shouldn't be told anything that we don't want the whole world to know. We have seen gossip spread like wildfire through a dry forest and have witnessed the effects of it. Every woman I meet comes with a default setting that she can't be trusted with information, and then she earns my trust from there. Men, on the other hand, start out with full trust, and then can lose it with severe consequences.

I know many people are rolling their eyes right now thinking I'm making a super-sexist generalization, but how many of us haven't witnessed women telling stories that they absolutely should not be sharing? Do guys gossip? Yes. Do we do it about things that matter? No. Women use information, and especially inside information, as a currency to create intimacy with other women. "I shouldn't be telling you this, but I know you'll keep it a secret." Ever uttered this statement? You started using it in high school and haven't stopped. I know what a lot of you are thinking: I never talk at work about the people there. Okay, but do you tell your spouse or family what is going on? Men call this bridge gossip. It is plausible that men tell their wives what is going on at business, but it is always told in confidence. I share things with Jacqui with the understanding that she is the only one who knows and that there are consequences if she spills her guts to someone else. That being said, she doesn't hear the sensitive stuff because there is no benefit to her knowing it, and men, unlike women, don't get giddy over knowing a secret. It is more of a burden to us. I know from female friends of mine who is sleeping with whom in their company, what new projects they are going after, who is getting fired, and who is getting headhunted. I may not be in the company, but I know people in the company, and I now have information I shouldn't be privy to. As a rapport builder, it probably works well. As a credibility killer, it works exponentially better. This is a fast track to getting deep-sixed by an Alpha Male.

Men have a code that women have heard about but don't fully understand. The code includes things like you don't talk disrespectfully about another guy's family, you don't sleep with his sister or any girl that he has ever dated, and above all else you don't snitch. There are two types of guys in jail who are in protective custody: child molesters and snitches. In an Alpha Male's eyes, the two are almost the same. I know that is a very contentious thing to say, but men have to be able to trust others in order to get things done. If someone gives me their word that they are going to keep something quiet and they don't, I want blood. I want to punish them so severely that they will assume the hand of God has come down from the heavens and crushed their life. That's pretty brutal, but in reality a man is only as good as his word, and if he not only breaks his word to me, but shares sensitive information of mine with others, I need retribution. I expect him to keep my confidence; whereas I expect women to tell everything we talk about to their friends, sisters, coworkers, husbands, and anyone else who might find it interesting.

Alpha Males set up women to see if they can keep a secret. We call it "sending up test balloons" when we give a woman a story that is completely false and ask her not to tell anyone. Then we wait and see if we hear any remnants of the story back from others. It is normally something that I can easily say is false and prove that it is false, thus discrediting the person who shared the story and not myself. She can't come back to me and give me hell for it because she knew it was a secret, so I just leave her out there to hang. If she does keep the secret, now I start with half truths. Again these have enough about the story wrong to discredit her to peers. When I speak to a woman and I'm sending a test balloon, I make it clear to her that it isn't common knowledge and there is a competitive advantage to us holding this information close. Here is an example:

If I'm closing a big deal, I might tell her that we are losing money and considering laying people off. I ask her not to say anything because I'm making my final decision. Because there is a big deal coming in, a layoff is the exact opposite of what any business owner would do, and I'm in a strong position if she betrays my trust. Then I wait and leave her out there to see if she is loyal to me or more loyal to the people who work for me. If it does get back to me, I dismiss it and she looks like *Henny Penny* running around saying the sky is falling, and I again leave her out there to hang. If she comes to me to inquire about the different messages, I will grill her as to why she thinks it important to share things I tell her in confidence, then I deep-six her. You give me your word and break it and the consequences will be great.

If on the somewhat rare occasion that I tell a woman something that is a lie and she keeps it, and then she keeps a half-truth, I will start giving her small truths—nothing too damaging, but things I might not want everyone to know. If she keeps these, I allow her in the inner circle and speak freely with her. This puts her in a very strong position because she begins to know everything and can be very dangerous if she leaves the circle.

There are some key points to remember when it comes to managing information:

1. The information is not yours; it's the person's who gave it to you. Hold it with respect.
2. You have broken your promise of secrecy even if you tell someone who will never come into contact with the situation.

3. Once you have broken this trust, every man will know that you can't be trusted and will look for ways to deep-six you to get you out of their way in case you come across some of their private information.

4. The keeper of secrets is the most important and powerful person in any circle. Become this person and you will position yourself to call in favors down the road.

5. Any time you think about sharing a secret, consider allowing someone to read from your journal aloud in front of your coworkers. This is what you are doing to someone else.

There are a couple of exceptions to this: if someone's physical safety is in danger or if crimes are being committed (think Enron). I'm not talking about if someone is going to lose his or her job or not get promoted. I mean serious danger to them. Even though it is snitching, I think you need to be able to live with yourself and do the right thing for you.

Last year I went into a pub in Vancouver and saw Jacqui's hair stylist sitting at the bar with a guy who was not her boyfriend. I know her boyfriend from being at the same parties, and when I saw her cozy with another guy I just walked by her. She called out my name and I just kept on walking. I wasn't mad that she was cheating on her boyfriend; I just didn't want to be involved in keeping a secret from him. Jacqui went to see her a few weeks later, and she asked Jacqui why I would have ignored her. Jacqui asked about the situation and found out that she had been out on a date with a new boyfriend as she and the old guy had broken up a few months before. Jacqui shared with her that, if this was the case, I probably wanted to avoid the situation so I could plead the fifth if I was ever asked about it. I never even told Jacqui what I saw because it wasn't my story to share. When in doubt, keep your mouth shut. No good comes out of having loose lips, especially in business. Remember that all Alphas assume that you are going to spill your guts so when you prove us wrong, you get a first-class seat in the inner circle of our business lives. If you tell our stories, you will experience difficulty from all directions. It will always come back to bite you in the ass.

11

Lost at Sea: Bringing Personal Issues to Work

Have you ever done the following at work:

1. Come in tired from a late night out?
2. Talked about an illness in your family?
3. Discussed a problem you are having at home?
4. Talked about a boyfriend or spouse and any issues you were having?
5. Talked about fears, insecurities, things that happened to you, your history, your time growing up, and so on?
6. Described what you did on the weekend or what you are planning to do on your vacation?

The workplace is for work. It isn't a place to go for solace from your personal life, it isn't a place to go for support when life is getting tough, and it isn't a place where you share aspects of your personal life with colleagues. It is a place where you are paid to develop, manage, or create something. But because professionals are spending more time at work then ever before, the line between personal life and professional life gets blurred.

Many people see their colleagues more hours per week than their family. That being said, it is important for you to be two-faced: to have a professional persona and a personal persona. These two faces should not be in conflict with each other, but they also shouldn't share space in your life. One way to undermine yourself to male counterparts is to bring personal issues to work.

There are four main consequences of bringing issues to work: It is unprofessional, it invites meddlers, it undermines your credibility to get work done, and it makes everyone around you uncomfortable.

It Is Unprofessional

There is an expectation of professionalism when you are in a professional setting. I don't buy into the traditional business expectations on how one is to act in business, but my rule is never to lose my cool or show emotion in front of those who aren't close to me. It isn't something that I think professional contacts need to know. When I'm at work, I'm focused on work. If I wake up on the wrong side of the bed, if I was out late the night before, if I'm having a stressful time, I keep all these things to myself. It is nobody's business except mine. If you broadcast your personal life, you open yourself up to outside judgments. If you are fighting with your husband, your kids just got kicked out of school, or your mom is ill, all this information is personal and should be kept that way.

It Invites Meddlers

Every business group has individuals who just look for reasons to come to someone's aid. Most of these people have good intentions, but others are looking for fuel to keep the rumor mill going. If you offer personal information, you might as well send out invitations for meddlers to come up with their prescription on how you can fix your problem. Why even go here? Unless you are searching for attention, there is absolutely no reason to use professional contacts to solve a personal problem. Keep your private life private.

It Undermines Your Credibility to Get Work Done

Whether or not your personal issues have an affect on your ability to produce, everyone will assume they are affecting your workload. In business you want to do things that showcase your strength as a professional, not highlight the challenges you are facing. Again, the sharing of personal information is a reputation killer. You need to keep your image at work as being that of a professional, not someone who likes to pass the day shooting the breeze about non-business-related things.

Makes Others Uncomfortable

The last thing anyone wants to hear in business is how your dad had a heart attack, that your marriage isn't working, or that you think your kid is smoking pot. Even if it is ripping you up inside, keep it private. When you share your information with others, especially men, what pops into our heads is, "Why do I care?" I know that sounds rough, but we all have challenges of our own. What makes you think that we care about what is going on? We care about your ability to uphold your responsibilities so that we don't have to cover for you. Men are total liars to female colleagues when issues like this surface. Let me give you an example:

You: "Things are tough right now. My dad just had a heart attack, and I am trying to help my mom take care of him on the weekends."

Me: "That's too bad. I know that must be a lot of work. I hope your dad is feeling better soon."

But what I really want to say is, "Can we just get on to talking about the project? If you can't finish this project, let me know and I'll find someone who can. Jeez, I'm tired of hearing this crap. When my dad had cancer, you didn't see me running around looking for sympathy! I wish we could get past the small talk and get to business."

I can't say what I think because that would make me a cold-hearted bastard. Women make men uncomfortable with these conversations. We don't care about your personal life, we don't care about your dad, and we don't really care about the outcome.

All we care about is how your personal life is going to affect you in a professional setting and how, in turn, that is going to affect us. Your personal life is your personal life. If for some reason you can't work effectively due to personal issues, don't come to work.

Here's a little secret: Men have days where we don't want to get out of bed and we know that we can't face colleagues and put on a convincing show. Rather than being scrutinized and having people pry into our lives, we immediately catch the flu and take a few days to get control of the situation. Having the ability to separate your two lives is a powerful tool for professionals to have at their disposal. It becomes a bit of a defense mechanism. I remember when my dad was first diagnosed with cancer. It was tough on me, but I didn't let on to anybody. There are few people in my professional circle who know anything about my personal life. I must keep them separate to preserve the good in both.

12

You're Waving and Drowning: Seeking External Affirmation

Have you ever ...

1. Asked an Alpha Male boss for feedback?
2. Asked a male colleague how he thought you did?
3. Asked for a male colleague to check your work to make sure you are doing it right.
4. Asked for objective feedback on how you do your job?

The need for external affirmation is something that everyone in business experiences, but men are experts at concealing it. Simply stated, external affirmation is the need to have an opinion other than your own to give credit to your actions. When men hear women looking for compliments, we think that the woman is totally weak and needs us to give a nod so that she feels better.

Men look for affirmation differently. First of all, we compare our actions to those around us and determine where we are in the pecking order. From there, if we are stronger than the others, we have our affirmation. If we obviously aren't, we then look for an area where we are stronger than

119

everyone else and keep that in our mind. We have a "kiss my ass" attitude when it comes to how others see us. It's a contrived mindset that we put in place to protect ourselves from criticism. Women don't seem to have this safeguard mechanism hot-wired in and look for affirmation from external sources.

The problem most men have with women who look for affirmation is that, in our minds, if you are good you shouldn't need someone else to tell you. The weakest of the group typically needs the most coddling. To us, looking for affirmation is the same as admitting weakness. Men not only hate weakness, but we try to distance ourselves from it as much as possible. Have you ever seen a man around a crying woman? He can't get far enough away. Aside from men judging those who seek affirmation as weak, we also think that you are doing it for a bunch of other reasons, including getting us to tell you to buy into something, looking for someone to answer something for you and do your work, or looking for an alliance in case something goes sideways. All of these perceived motivations undermine you as a business professional.

Checking to See If Something Is a Good Idea

When you ask us what we think of your idea, project, or actions, we think that you are trying to get us to tell you if you are on the right path or not. If you say something like, "I was going to go chat with the regional director about a promotion. Do you think that the timing is right?" We hear, "I'm going to ask for a raise. Do you think I'm worth it?" We'll say to you, "Sure!" but we are saying to ourselves, "If you were worth it, you wouldn't have to ask!"

Looking to Have Others Answer Your Questions

Sometimes when you look for external affirmation, we think that you might be looking for us to do some of your work for you.

If you say, "Do you think that going after the Anderson account should be a priority for my department, instead of focusing on the Smith account?" we hear, "Hi, I don't know how to do my job, and I need to be micromanaged. Can you do that for me and point me in the right direction?" If you ask this question as a sober second thought, a better way to approach it is to say, "I've done research on the opportunities with the

Anderson account, and I'm leaning towards putting more energy towards it. Being so close to it, I wouldn't mind a second opinion that is objective. Any thoughts pop into your head?"

What you are doing here is letting the guy know that you have done your homework and you want someone on the outside to have a quick look with fresh eyes.

Looking to Form Alliances

As mentioned previously, when women attack in the workplace they often seek people who agree with their point and justify their actions. If you go to a man with any issue, to find out what his thoughts are, he will smile, nod, decide that you are dangerous, and start the process of deep-sixing you. Here are some examples of things women will say that will lead men to start the process:

- "I am so tired of our boss not following through with our job reviews. Do you think we should say something to the regional director?"
- "Jerry is a total jerk. I wonder if I should write an anonymous letter to the manager. Do you think I should?"
- "Is it just me or would getting rid of Debbie on this project make things go much better?"
- "I'm tired of being here. I think I'm going to take off without notice. Do you think that's a good idea?"

When we hear comments like this we know that you are looking for an accomplice so that if trouble hits the fan you can bring us into the mix as having agreed with your actions. We don't like it when people pick fights for us; we prefer to pick our own fights.

13

Who Deserves a Spot in the Lifeboat?: Expecting Fairness in Business

Have you ever ...

1. Openly wondered why you aren't getting promoted?
2. Trained subordinates to become superiors?
3. Waited for someone to notice your contributions?
4. Not asked for a raise feeling that they will fairly compensate you?
5. Been passed over for projects that you knew you were perfect for?
6. Wondered why you are passed over for committee involvement?
7. Said in mixed company that you thought something was unfair?
8. Pointed out injustices in the workplace?
9. Used the terms "fair" and "equal" in the workplace?

Throughout my professional career, the most unsettling fact that I have experienced is that there is a lack of integrity in how people do business. I have met many more people looking to make a quick buck than those who are truly interested in being in the market long term and providing a great service or exceptional product. Business is a pure model of engagement that gets tainted by personalities. In its simplest form, business is a transaction involving two or more parties in which one trades something of value for something else of comparable value.

Problems arise with the exchange of these items of value. Business is not inherently fair, and a good majority of those you meet in business will be looking for an advantage wherever they can get it. You are reading this book because you want to have an advantage over others who have not.

Business is based on selfishness. Once you can understand and accept that fact, you can get past the idealistic approach that business is fair. Anyone who tells you differently is either lying or doesn't know any better.

There are three main beliefs that put women in a position to get burnt by someone because they haven't accepted that business isn't always fair. Following are the beliefs that challenge women.

Assuming That Everyone Shares the Same Rules

The individuals you do business with, whether it is your boss, your partner, your colleague, your client, your supplier or others, will have learned how to do business in their own way and married that to their integrity, belief system, and other factors that influence one's actions.

What I'm getting at is that none of us does business the same way; some will do things very similarly, while others couldn't be more different from you. This means that the rules with which you govern yourself will not necessarily be the rules that others follow.

When I first started in business I came from the school where it was exciting to try to knock competitors out of business. I'm talking about literally trying to bankrupt them. Because I went through some transitions, I now can't believe how I used to think. I now think of all competitors as colleagues because there are plenty of clients for everyone and we will all do things differently. What you consider to be right will be considered wrong by others and vice versa; it may also evolve and change as your career progresses. Accept this and know it to be the truth. You can't expect others to follow your rules unless you tell them what they are and they agree to them.

Assuming That Everyone Is Looking Out for Everyone

Nobody is going to watch your back for you except you. Friends in business may give each other a heads up, but no one is going to be as interested in keeping you out of harm's way as much as you are. Consider a downsizing situation. People get axed, and everyone talks to each other about how valuable an asset each member of the team is.

This is all show. Everyone is really thinking, "I'd fire her, she doesn't do anything anyway!" We all have our own best interest at heart, yet we pretend that we are the selfless martyrs looking to take care of each other. Remember, you are (or should be) your own biggest fan. Do not expect anyone else to make sure you have a place at the dinner table.

If you are counting on others to protect your interests, you are going to be sadly disappointed. Fairness only occurs if it doesn't jeopardize the other individuals. Your friends will sell you out if it's between you or them. It sounds harsh, and you might think that this isn't representative of the friendships you have, but trust me it is extremely important to err on the side of being overly cautious rather than flagrantly trusting.

Assuming That Everyone Has the Same Passion for the Project

When you are working on a project that you are really excited about, don't expect everyone else to share your excitement. When professionals get involved in a project (either by their own initiative or due to professional responsibility), they are thinking about how the project can benefit them. Could it lead to some strong contacts? Could it lead to a promotion? Is it a waste of time?

We all ask these questions when we are involved in a project, but men pay particular attention to the strategic benefit of their involvement. If we can't see how it benefits us, we will play along but you will have a hard time getting us excited. Get over it. If we don't see personal gain, you probably won't convince us on the project's merit. We most likely won't do our fair share of the work, so plan for this.

You can guard yourself somewhat to these unfair situations by ensuring that rules are discussed prior to needing to enforce them. Men call these agreements "rules of engagement." I want to share with you that men have certain agreements that are bred into us. We will cross a woman 10 times quicker than we will another man because repercussions from a woman are rare and minimal as opposed to those from men.

Here are some of the rules men agree to without discussing. I follow these rules with every man I know, but I've never had a discussion with them about these rules.

1. I will not go after you in a professional setting unless I'm prepared to go head to head with you till the death (overly dramatic, but appropriate).

2. I understand that if you embarrass me, I will need to look over my shoulder as long as we are in the same market space.
3. I understand that if I take one of your clients, you will look for ways till the end of time to take all my clients and discredit me.
4. We are stronger together then we are apart, so we'll respect our collective expertise and hunt together.
5. You will not disrespect me knowing that I'm a mover and at some time in the future you may have to eat your words with me.
6. I will keep my word with you, as I know you will judge me solely on my ability to deliver for you. I want my word to be strong with you so that your word is strong with me.
7. I will support you and promote you as long as it is never above me.
8. I don't work for you; I work with you.
9. At anytime you think I'm not a closer/hunter/winner, I know that you will quietly move away from me and I will do the same to you.
10. If you get caught doing something inappropriate, I will protect you to the extent it starts to affect me, then I'll cut you loose.

Men and women rarely have this conversation with each other, but we really should. When we are all on the same page, we will be respectful of each other's positions. With all my clients, I go over my rules of engagement with them straightaway so that they know my rules and the rules I want them to follow if they want to work with me.

Establishing boundaries is basically letting others know what rules you have that they must respect if they want to interact with you. That brings me to an important point: You can't control how people act or the rules that they govern themselves by, but you can control how they interact with you. By letting them know what your boundaries are, they gain clarity on what your expectations are and what you will not tolerate. They can do those things, but just not with you.

Sample Rules of Engagement

1. Cell phones must be turned off during meetings. If you can't miss a call, don't come to the meeting. If you can't turn off your phone, I can't make time for you.
2. No badmouthing other professionals in front of me. I don't want to be associated with professionals who slam their competition.

3. You will tell me the truth. If I find out you lied to me, our business relationship is finished. You can lie, just not to me.
4. You will be on time for our meetings. I don't care if you aren't on time for anything else, if you are late for me, I won't meet with you.

You should make a list of all the rules you have for yourself and then build a list of boundaries that you will have for others. Here are a few examples:

Rule	Boundary
"I will always be on time."	"In order for me to meet with someone, they must be on time."
"I will tell the truth."	"In order to do business with me, you must always tell me the truth."

Try to come up with as many as you can, and when you are doing business with someone let them know what your expectations are and ask them what theirs are. I wouldn't say, "Here are my boundaries and follow them or we aren't doing business." Instead, I'd suggest you say, "I want to make sure that you and I are on the same page with expectations. What are your requirements of people you do business with?" Once they have the opportunity to tell you, then you can add the ones that you have that they didn't bring up.

This is most powerful in negotiations. Imagine what your negotiations would look like if you said the following:

"Let's agree before we start that this process is going to end with either a win-win situation or we simply won't be able to work together. I don't want either of us to get the short straw, so let's both ensure we are making this deal work for both of us. I'd sooner not have a deal with you than for either of us to feel we didn't get what we wanted. Do you agree?"

As soon as you state your boundaries, any strategies the other party had in mind to take a dominant position are out the window because you have been clear with your expectations and they know that you are prepared to leave rather than to have a bad deal. Both parties will now look at how to build a good deal for everyone involved, as opposed to focusing on not getting screwed.

14

Abandon Ship: Accepting Poor Treatment

Have you ever . . .

1. Gone home after a hard day at work feeling you were treated unfairly?
2. Felt that you were singled out for discipline?
3. Been spoken to without respect?
4. Been reprimanded publicly?
5. Been treated poorly by someone and then made an excuse why they did it?
6. Felt like you were talked over or dismissed verbally in a meeting?
7. Had your ideas shot down?

One of the most challenging things that women face in a business setting is how to deal with male counterparts who treat them poorly. I'm not talking about when they say something offensive, although speaking offensively is part of it. Ultimately, I am talking about being treated like a pest, a child, or a subordinate and being spoken to in a condescending, judging, or disrespectful tone.

If you accept poor treatment as a cost of having the job (which I have heard more than once), you are not only doing yourself a grave disservice, but you are setting the tone for what is acceptable for your female coworkers and those who follow in your footsteps.

Before you can deal with the issue you need to understand that, as an adult and a qualified professional, you have the ability to respond; hence you can take responsibility for what is going on and what is going to happen in the future. Let me share with you the reasoning that I most often hear when women tell me about a disrespectful male counterpart and why they think he acts that way. Professional women have become experts at rationalizing why men do the things they do. Almost always they are wrong in their assessment and allow themselves to be mistreated without reason. Here are four common reactions I've observed in professional women.

Making Excuses for Why People Act Up

When a coworker does something disrespectful to a woman, if she doesn't go head to head right off the bat she will begin the tedious (and unnecessary) process of determining why she thinks that person acted the way he did. She goes back in her memory searching for anything she may have said that could have contributed to his acting out.

Do any of these responses sound familiar?

- "He is going through a divorce right now and is just stressed."
- "I think he is having problems at home with his kids."
- "He got passed up for that promotion."
- "He's frustrated with how the project is going."
- "He's been working long hours."

When you make excuses for others' actions, you condone their actions. *Do not do this*! As I said earlier, personal issues should never influence professional matters. There are no excuses for poor treatment of others in the workplace, so don't look for them.

Considering It an Isolated Incident

If you find you are the brunt of poor treatment and the person who treated you that way doesn't have a history of it, do not consider it an isolated incident and treat it as water under the bridge. It is important that everyone sees you aren't a pushover or a tackling dummy when someone feels like striking out verbally. Even if you are treated poorly only once, it is one time too many. Deal with it immediately.

Not Wanting to Make Things Worse

Most women do not enjoy conflict. Most men, on the other hand, love conflict, and we passively or aggressively seek it out at times. Regardless of your feelings towards conflict, know that you will not necessarily create more by addressing the issue. This is not about you making him wrong and you right. It is about acknowledging what happened and ensuring that it won't happen again.

Assuming This Is Just Something You Have to Accept to Get Ahead

Let me be extremely clear here: Poor treatment is not something you have to learn to deal with in order to get ahead. You don't have to take hits to show you are strong. You have a choice. You can take the poor treatment, sulk about it, let it influence your work environment, take those issues home with you, and make yourself miserable. Or you can address the situation and ensure that others are very clear on what your boundaries are.

At this point, you are probably thinking, "Yes, I know that I should address it, but how do I do it without getting deep-sixed and bringing more conflict onto myself?" My suggestion is to deal with the issue immediately, concisely, and professionally. The issue has to be identified without taking it personally and boundaries have to be formed. For example:

Tina is working for an ad agency in Boston. During a strategic meeting, Tina brings up an issue that isn't directly related to the discussion, but she feels will have an outcome on the goal. The meeting is three hours in and nerves are getting a little raw. Her team leader turns to her and he says, "For Chrissakes Tina, can you please keep on task here? I don't want to have to keep pulling you along! Get in the game, or go find something else to do." This is a pretty tough statement and an overreaction. Her team leader is showing his frustration and verbally strikes out at her. The group is shocked and looks to quickly get back on task to get past the awkwardness of the situation.

Tina has a few options. She can get past it and realize that he is just stressed out and it wasn't good timing on her part. She can pretend it didn't happen. She can just let it go. She can take a run at him right there in front of the group and tell him that he is unprofessional. Or, she can make the decision to address his actions directly after the meeting. My suggestion is the latter.

Directly after the meeting, she should go up to him and say, "We need to have a private discussion right now." This will put him on his heels, and he either will agree to have the discussion or he'll try to dodge her knowing what is coming. Either way, she has just taken her power back. If he dodges the meeting, she should find him and state, "We need to set up a time to have a talk today. Get back to me by lunch time." When she does get to speak with him, it is important to be very clear without making him wrong.

Tina should say: "I need to be extremely clear with you. Regardless of the situation, I am always to be talked to with the utmost respect. I will never be talked to like that again. I want us to be very clear on that."

Then she can leave. She doesn't need to hear his excuses or comments. He now has the information that she needs him to have. She should not do this by e-mail or phone. It must be done in person. E-mail and phone allow either party to distance himself from the situation.

You have a responsibility to yourself and all female colleagues to ensure that boundaries are put in place so male counterparts know that they treat female colleagues with the same respect and in the same manner that they treat their male colleagues.

Remember: It is never okay to accept poor treatment! A woman who accepts poor treatment without addressing it is as guilty as the man committing the injustice. When you allow it to happen or give it an excuse, you are telling every other woman that it is simply a price you need to pay to be a woman in business. That is total bullshit. Address it without making the guy wrong and do so in private. Remember, you don't have to make him wrong to be right. You do have to set boundaries and, in turn, will set boundaries on behalf of other women in your organization.

15

"Let Me Do All the Rowing": Trying to Be Liked and Selfless

Have you ever ...

1. Done things because you think people will like you?
2. Talked about topics you aren't interested in but know the other person likes?
3. Helped out with work that wasn't yours to show that you are a team player?
4. Taken on others' assignments on short notice?
5. Offered to help a coworker move, return phone calls, do research, or other helpful things?
6. Done chores or tasks you aren't responsible for to help someone else out?

In business, the first thing that you want from anyone you do business with is respect. Many women focus on building rapport with their colleagues and clientele, which is important, but it is not the most important thing. I would much rather be respected than liked. The challenge women face in business is to break the stereotypes that people have about women in business. Women are expected to be friendly and giving. Most women fill this stereotype. For those who don't want to fit this role, they often over compensate by being bitchy. Neither serves you.

What you want to do is practice selfish self-protection. I want you to make a list of everything that you need to have, to give to others openly and without regret. Women approach this backwards. They practice selfless self-sabotage. This means that they care for everyone else and then try to find time to do what they need to for themselves. Does this sound familiar to you? Let me give you an example of the two different ways of approaching this.

Selfless Self-Sabotage

Colleague: "Lisa, I really need some help with this report that is due tomorrow. I have meetings all day, and I need some support to get this deal closed. Could you run over to the library and pick up those documents for me? It would be really helpful."

Lisa: "I'm really swamped, but I can make a quick run over to help you out. Is that all you need to get the report in?"

Lisa thinks that she is being a team player by helping to achieve the goal of the project. What she isn't sharing is that she has responsibilities that are due the next day as well, but wanting to be seen in a positive manner, she thinks that she has to say yes to be respected and liked by her colleague. Plus, she is sure he will help her out sometime in the future when she needs it (wrong!).

She is putting others before herself; this is going to take more away from her than just time. It is going to add stress to her workload. Because she is going to be at work later, she also has sacrificed some of her free time. And if she doesn't get it done, she has just become the scapegoat for the project.

Selfish Self-Protection

Colleague: "Lisa, I really need some help with this report that is due tomorrow. I have meetings all day, and I need some support to get this deal closed. Could you run over to the library and pick up those documents for me? It would be really helpful."

Lisa: "Tim, I'm sorry but I can't support you right now. I have reports that I need to have in tomorrow morning as well. What about asking Tom or Tina to give you a hand? Next time, if you can give me a little more notice, I'd be happy to help if time allows."

She has put herself first and let him know that he can't drop work on her at the last minute. Also, by letting him know that she has responsibilities that also need to be completed, she tells him that she takes her responsibilities seriously. He will now be educated that she isn't a pile-on for work that he doesn't have time to do.

Nice people are attractive to Alpha Males because they are who we dump our work onto, especially the stuff that we don't want to do or that we have left till the last minute. We know that nice people have a hard time saying no to our requests. If you are one of these nice people, you probably notice that not only does the same person give you more and more things to help with, but also now more and more people are seeking your help. This is because when we find someone who will do our work, we tell other Alphas about it.

Example of Alpha Male conversation about nice female counterparts:

Alpha #1: "I've left this damn project till the last minute, and I need to get it done so that I can close this deal."

Alpha #2: "Just ask Jennifer to help you out. She can prep all the work, and all you need to do is look over it."

This is how we talk among ourselves. We don't say, "Give it to her, she is a pleaser." We always use language that is defendable. Imagine if it ever came back to the Alpha Male that he had said that comment about Jennifer, he would easily defend it by saying, "Yes, I said to ask Jennifer. I have always found her very effective in helping out when I'm in a pinch." It isn't judgmental, and it doesn't sound bad objectively, but when two Alpha Males are talking the understanding is deeper than the meaning when we are talking about nice people.

Nice people don't finish last, pleasers do.

16

"Here, You Take the Last Life Preserver": Asking for What You Want

Have you ever . . .

1. Thought about what you wanted, but thought it unrealistic?
2. Really wanted something but were unsure how to ask for it?
3. Thought you deserved a raise, but didn't want to make the situation uncomfortable?
4. Asked for a promotion because you have been loyal?
5. Looked at the price of something you needed for business and decided to ask for something cheaper?
6. Worked in a position where you know a male colleague with the same experience is making more?

Men ask for more than they deserve; women ask for what they think is reasonable. Most women I have encountered have a voice in their head talking through what they are worth. This voice is the critic and keeps a woman from asking for what she wants. If a man and a woman are in equal positions making $50,000 a year, the guy will ask for $90,000 and tell why he is worth it. The woman will ask for

$55,000 because she thinks it's reasonable and won't make the other party uncomfortable.

Women need to get clear on what it is they want rather than what they think they can get. Using wages as an example, I've never met an Alpha Male who works for a company and isn't clear to the dollar how much he makes for his company. He has done all the math and knows what his remuneration is as a percentage of the business he brings in. We do this not only to have a measurement against our counterparts, but also to have a negotiation chip for salary discussions. Women don't seem to do this as much. They want to be reasonable, fair, and unpretentious. They don't want to showboat or be greedy. When a company is making a whack of dough off of you, you should get paid well because you are an asset.

I have a client who has worked for four years in a pretty sizeable Los Angeles law firm. She decided to take on business development as one of her roles and is the only associate who opens up files on a regular basis. She has consistently opened up at least three files a month for two years. The only other people with that consistency are senior partners (Finders). When the associates have their yearly review, they are asked by the managing partners to submit a proposal on what they think their bonus should be. My client was the only woman to do this because the other female associates chose to allow the partners to decide what was fair. My client got a bonus four times that of any other associate because she asked for a number and justified how it was just a small percentage of the work she had brought in, not to mention that she met or exceeded both her hourly and financial targets. If her female colleagues had done the same, even without the business development, they probably would have received double their bonuses.

When it comes to asking for raises, the Alpha asks for more than he deserves and fights for it, while the female floats a number up and always gets it. This is a real world example. Let me show you how it turned out, and keep in mind both did basically the same amount of work.

| *Man* | *Making $50K* | *Asked for $90K* | *Got $68K* |
| *Woman* | *Making $50K* | *Asked for $55K* | *Got $55K* |

This is why there is a gender discrepancy in income levels. Men ask for more and get it. It's not a riddle, it's simply asking for what you want. I know two chamber of commerce managers in British Columbia who oversee organizations of equal size, with similar membership numbers, and with almost identical budgets. The man makes $70,000 a year, and the woman makes $53,000 a year. The difference in pay is because the man's board knows he won't work for $53,000, and the woman's board knows she will. This is a supply-side dynamic. If women won't work for less, they won't have to. Women need to continue the selfish self-protection, get really clear on what they want, not what they think they can get, and ask for it!

17

"Life Boats in the Back": Developing a Plan B

Have you ever ...

1. Found yourself fired without another job opportunity?
2. Felt stuck in a situation because you didn't have other options?
3. Felt like you were just putting in time waiting for things to get better?
4. Dreaded going to work or seeing a challenging client?

Plan B—that's a term guys use to refer to our backup plans. We spend a lot of our day coming up with contingencies in case things don't go our way. When I got married, I thought about what I'd do if I got divorced. When I close a big client, I think about whom I can replace them with if they don't pay. When I hire an assistant, I think of who can take their spot if I let him or her go. I have hidden keys for my car and house in case I get locked out. I have backup credit cards, cash on hand, and so on just in case. Men commit a lot of time to hoping for the best and planning for the worst. By doing so, we always have options. If we know a client might be going sideways, we start conversations with their competitors so that if we fire the client we can try to pull the trigger on their competitor and instantaneously replace income. If we have a shitty boss, we start talking with our network looking at opportunities that we can move into. By having a Plan B, we ensure we are nobody's bitch. We will do things our way or walk. Women, on the other hand, are so busy taking care of their husbands, family, coworkers, friends, and the like that they don't come up with a Plan B. Then if the shit hits the fan, they are caught without a map.

I joke with crowds that when a ship is sinking, after the rats have jumped off and the crew is in lifeboats, the woman is helping the captain get his jacket on to make sure that he stays warm for the trip. Do you think Alphas will do that for you? No! We will downsize, fire, replace, sabotage, or deep-six you whenever it selfishly benefits us. If you do not having a backup plan, you allow us to have extra power over you. We can threaten you with your job, especially if you are breadwinner, because we know finding a job tomorrow will be tough. Let me give you an example:

Option 1—Woman with No Plan B

Boss: "Brenda, I've been looking at our sales remuneration on commissions and decided to change it. I'm dropping it from 20 percent to 10 percent effective next Monday."

Brenda: "Okay, but that is going to make it very difficult for me to cover my monthly expenses, do you have any suggestions on how I can get my sales up?"

Brenda is at the will of her boss. She will accept it and might start looking for another job, but probably will first think how she can sell more stuff to get her commissions back up. Basically she has to figure out a way to sell double what she has been just to be at the same point. At this point Brenda gets bitter and in most cases will wonder what she did wrong and question her value in business.

Now let's just assume that Brenda has been working on developing a network of people and has showed visibility, credibility, and profitability to colleagues. She will start to get job offers or, at the very least, hear about other companies that would like to have her on board. Brenda's Plan B is a contact at another company who has said to her, "We will be competitive in remuneration to get you over here. You have a position any time you want one."

Option 2—Woman with a Plan B

Now when her boss tells her that her commission structure is changing, this is her response:

Boss: "Brenda, I've been looking at our sales remuneration on commissions and decided to change it. I'm dropping it from 20 percent to 10 percent effective next Monday."

Brenda: "I'm sorry, but that isn't going to fit for me. As a performer for this company, I actually need my commission to rise to 30 percent with a car allowance, or I'm going to accept another offer that has been made to me. Please consider it until Monday. If this isn't possible, consider my resignation submitted, and I'll give you two weeks notice unless you would like it to be less."

Brenda is in the driver's seat. She is nobody's bitch. If the game doesn't fit for her, she simply changes the way she plays it. She can only do this effectively because she has a Plan B that allows her to make a lateral move. A Plan B is insurance. You may work for a great company or have great clients, but if something goes sideways that you can't control you want to have options immediately available to you. A Plan B is time well spent.

Here is what I have my clients do as a step-by-step process for developing their Plan B:

- Identify the situation (job, client, relationship, whatever)
- Determine the worst-case scenario
- Decide what steps you would take if you found yourself in that situation tomorrow
- Make a list of the steps you can take now as insurance in case this happens
- What would have to be available to you to feel like you were insulated

Here is an example of how someone might develop their Plan B:

- *Situation:* Have a client in oil and gas who we bill $300,000 a year on marketing services.
- *Worst-case scenario:* Clients leave and take their business with them due to bankruptcy, change in management, hiring in-house advisers.
- *If this happened, I would:* make a list of all the other companies of comparable size and in similar market space and begin chatting with them and showcasing our services and experience.
- *Steps I can take today:* make a list of who these companies are with their contact people. Research their contact people and find out their backgrounds. Track their marketing opportunities and what I would do differently or more cost effectively. Attend industry events and introduce myself and get them warmed up.
- *I will know I'm insulated when:* one or more of them asks if we are taking on new clients or if we have time to sit down and talk strategy with them.

Follow this process and you, too, will have a plan that hopefully you won't have to use, but if you do, you will be prepared!

18

"Welcome Aboard!": Understanding Business Endorsements

Have you ever ...

1. Tried to get referrals from a colleague?
2. Made referrals to another business?
3. Had prospects come in that wasted your time?
4. Been burnt by someone who was referred to you?
5. Wondered why you get referrals, but few are qualified?
6. Had prospects come in only to realize that they weren't a fit or they didn't have money?

Why not finish off this book with something contentious? Referrals are mud! They are a mere suggestion, not an endorsement, and I have seen many a professional waste their time meeting with people who absolutely aren't a fit for their business. Alphas have a saying, "Earners are building networks while boat anchors are networking." A referral is a suggestion, the same as a television ad or a yellow pages advertisement. An endorsement is a referral's big daddy. When you look at key Alphas, like the character of Tony Soprano on the series *The Sopranos*, he doesn't refer people to do work with each other, he plays matchmaker. He also decides on a set of rules so that everyone is fair and happy. When they are, he looks good. If they aren't, he takes things into his own hands.

Women go to networking events and end up talking to the same women as the previous month. Some of the more adventurous ones will meet new people and either 1) try to make new friends or 2) try to pimp their services. We've all seen the boat anchor who attends one of these dinners and walks around the room putting her marketing pieces on everyone's plate or seat. That's equivalent to the idiot who puts the pizza flyer on my windshield at the mall. It goes right into the garbage as soon as possible. The person doing this is looking for referrals, but Alphas make a decision within a minute not to suggest her. Otherwise we would look just like the boat anchor. Remember, it's all about visibility, credibility, profitability. These three pieces are based on one fundamental fact: Alphas endorse people who make them look good and make them money. When we make an endorsement it is strategic, methodical, and selfish. We put deals together for people; we don't simply make a suggestion. Making suggestions (referrals) is for rookies. Let me give you an example of both a referral and an endorsement so you can see the absolute power of the latter.

The situation:

Let's say that my friend Fiona is a sales coach and my friend Robbie owns an online company. Robbie needs sales training to help grow his company.

The referral:

Robbie: "Chris, do you know any good sales trainers? I need to bring someone in to work with my team."

Chris: "Yeah, you should check out Fiona Walsh. She's a sales trainer I know. E-mail me for her info."

I bet a lot of your are saying to yourselves right now, "That sounds pretty good. I'll take as many of those as you can hand out." But what you don't realize is out of 100 of those, 90 will be mud (unqualified buyers who will waste your time).

Instead, when an Alpha does a business endorsement, we have done our homework on each party (more so on the supplier). We know who they are (visibility), we know they can perform (credibility, meaning the buyer has money to spend and the supplier can fulfill expectations), and that it can be a beneficial relationship (profitability, meaning the client gets what they want and the supplier makes money doing so).

Using the same situation, here is how a business endorsement happens:

Robbie: "Chris, do you know any good sales trainers? I need to bring someone in to work with my team."

Chris "Yeah, I have someone in particular that I suggest to my inner circle. She doesn't have time for a piker so you need to be serious if you want to work with her."

Robbie: "Tell me about her."

Chris: "She has taken companies from zero to $15 million in a 12-month period. She is exceptional both as a trainer and a coach, and her clients make a shitload of money after they implement her tools."

Robbie: "Sounds great, can you make an introduction?"

Chris: "She's $1,500 a day. Do you have a budget for that?"

Robbie: "If you say she is worth it, I'll allocate the funds."

Chris: "Okay, I'll make the introduction. Don't waste her time and pay your invoice on time. You fuck up and it reflects badly on me. Okay? I'll see if she'll make some time available to meet you. If you have any problem, call me first and I'll take care of it."

Robbie: "Sounds good. Thanks for the hookup."

Now that I have qualified the buyer and given him the background on her, he is ready to deal. Now I go to Fiona and have the following conversation:

Chris: "Fiona, I have a client for you. He is a dear friend of mine and a whale (big earner) of a businessman. He needs sales training for his team. I told him you were the best, and he wants to meet you."

Fiona: "Thanks, Chris, when would you like me to meet him?"

Chris: "As soon as possible. He is ready to deal. I need you to treat him like he is your only client, like he has the same last name as you. I want him to think that he is gold and that he thanks God every time he thinks of me making this endorsement. You need to blow him away with service and performance. If you do what I think you'll do, there will be much more work from both of us. I told him you were $1,500/day and he is prepared to pay it. Make sure you make me and yourself look good. If this goes sideways for any reason, it isn't going to be good for our relationship, so make sure you deliver. If you have any problem, call me first and I'll take care of it."

I know this sounds somewhat like a Mafioso, but what I am doing is cosigning their credibility in each other with my credibility. I'm saying that they don't have to worry because I have done the due diligence on each of them. If there is a problem, I'll get involved, and no one wants the guy bringing the deals in to be unhappy. In this model, there are no requests for proposal, project presentations, or any of the traditional processes that you go through when you are referred to someone. They don't need additional references because, if the client has faith in me, they know that I won't represent mud. And if something gets off the tracks, I'll take responsibility because I made the endorsement.

This is how men build business so quickly—some call it "vouching," but it really is endorsement. On the other side of this, if you are the one making the recommendation (i.e., making referrals to someone else) and they are mud, the person is going to smile and thank you for thinking of them, but internally think that you must be mud, too, because of the people you hang out with. Guys have sayings like, "Don't throw up wood," which means don't chase business that isn't there. Start to build your practice with endorsement both coming in and going out, and make sure that visibility/credibility/profitability is the foundation of these endorsements. And, they should be made by you selfishly; you will look good, get reciprocal business, and maybe make some money off the deal. Remember, referrals are for losers; endorsements are for earners. Next time you are at a networking function, look to see who is playing the role and who is building business. Building business with Alphas means giving endorsements and getting endorsements.

PART III

Common Questions That Women Ask

(If you have skipped all the pages previous to this, I understand.)

Questions about. . .

Men: What Makes a Strong Sailor?

Why do all the men at the water cooler stop talking when I arrive?

Let me start off by saying, they haven't been talking about you nor are they trying to exclude you. They have been trying to amuse each other and fit in. Men often create bonds with each other by being outrageous, obnoxious, and saying things that are not politically correct. They stopped talking because they were most likely saying something inappropriate for mixed company. Because of the increased awareness of sexual harassment in the workplace, men are overly cautious now of not saying anything that would be taken wrongly by female colleagues and clients. So when the men go quiet, they were saying something that would be considered inappropriate in mixed company. You can say, "Hey guys, I like jokes like that, let me in on it," but we won't because that joke could cost us $50,000, and there isn't anything funny enough to warrant that bill.

Why do men always want to be the leader?

Leadership is a very important part of the Alpha Male's career. We need to show not only that we can get the endorsement to be the leader but also that we can deliver when in that position. Alpha Males don't like to be told what to do. When we are the leader, we tell others what to do,

149

which is something we are very fond of. If you aren't at the head of the pack, you are at the will of someone else. That isn't a position we like to be in. You'll see an Alpha Male in the lead and the rest of the Alpha Males in the group will look to be the leader in one of the sub areas.

Here's an example of how Alphas divvy up leadership:

- Bob is the Alpha Male in charge of the sales presentation with his team
- Jon takes on responsibility to oversee research
- Bill takes on the responsibility of choosing the venue and managing the event
- Tom takes on managing the presentation's development

Each of these men working with Bob isn't saying that he will work on his area. Instead, they say that they will take responsibility or manage their area, hence assuming the lead in these areas. It's a little game we play with ourselves so that are egos can handle being told what to do. Often we'll volunteer what we are going to do right off the bat so that someone else can't assign us a task that we think beneath us. To an Alpha Male, if you aren't the leader, you are someone's bitch.

Why are men workaholics?

Allow me to make some generalizations that I am quick to defend. Women in western society are judged by the way they look. In our world, a woman who is thin and attractive has an advantage over women who aren't. One need only look at television, music, and magazines to see that we still have this archaic belief that there is only one way to be attractive.

Our society, unfortunately, supports this in every way possible. Our society also supports men's role in our culture. Men are the hunters. We bring the food in for everyone to eat. The best hunters are to be held in the highest of regard, while the ones who don't hunt effectively are chastised and ridiculed. For men, our looks don't matter as much as our ability to generate revenue (modern hunting). A man can be 900 pounds, with a 14-inch mole on the top of his head, and if he is a billionaire every supermodel will want him, every guy will want to be his friend, and he will be invited to all the parties. Men are judged by this society solely on our ability to make money.

It isn't enough for us to make money; we have to make more money than everyone else we know. We can't just provide for our families. We need to provide better for our families than any other man we know. Men are always assessing the pecking order and their position in it as compared to all the other men they know. We are workaholics not because we love our work (although this is the case in many men), but we love that our work makes us money, which allows us to provide a better quality of life for our families, which betters our position in the pecking order.

I know a guy who stays home with his daughter while his wife goes to work. This guy is pretty lazy as it is, but he has decided that he will stay home and raise their daughter while his wife is the breadwinner. Now before I say something that is going to make you boil, let me state a few facts.

I believe that every woman should be in a profession if she chooses to. I believe that women should make great money at what they do, and I don't have any problems with women making more than their husbands. I know that raising a child is a tremendous amount of work, and those parents raising their children often outwork their spouses working outside the house.

However, the guy I'm referring to is at the lowest level I can conceive on the food chain. I think his staying at home and expecting his wife to support him is disgusting. Would I think that if his wife stayed home and he was out working? No I wouldn't. But the belief that able-bodied men should be making money for their families is so hard-wired into my psyche, that this is something I can't get past. Objectively I know my feelings on this are old fashioned and chauvinistic. Yet I still feel loathing toward a man who opts not to provide for his family.

Why do men prefer dealing with men?

There's no drama. We can tell each other to piss off and there are no tears. Worst-case scenario is we walk outside and beat the shit out of each other, don't talk for a year, invite each other for a beer, and get back to work making money together. If I reject a male colleague in a deal and he shows weakness, he knows he loses my respect and every future deal I might ever do with him. A majority of my clients are female, and if I want more out of them, I say, "I know you can do better than this because I've seen you do better. What do we need to do to take this up a level?" I let them know what my expectations are of them and then offer to troubleshoot with them. With male clients, I have a different approach. One in particular sent me a proposal he was putting in. My response to him was, "This is a total piece of shit. Not only will they not give you the contract, but also they are going to blackball you from any future work in the country. Fix it and get it back to me. If you think it's shit, don't even send it to me." Now many of you reading will think that I'm being a hard ass, but an Alpha Male wants to know what the heck to do to hit the ball out of the park. He doesn't care about what isn't working. He cares about doing something that will make him look good and get him paid. I'm telling him that the crap he is handing in will kill his reputation and cost him money. I read somewhere that friends tease you to protect you from the ridicule of society. I am harder on other Alpha Males because I know that they can both take it and thrive from it. I want them to prove me wrong.

When women like honest feedback, it makes men uncomfortable because we don't believe that you really want to know what we are thinking. Fiona Walsh, one of the top coaches in my organization (what we refer to as a "Ghost CEO coach"), is an elite business coach specializing in sales. She and I were having a strategy session and discussing a heated topic. She asked me what I thought and I smiled. She said, "Come on, Flett, give it to me, I know what your holding back!" So I gave it to her with both barrels—everything I didn't like about the idea, the delivery, the strategy, the profit model, and the implementation. She sat there and took it all in, and I was ready for some type of drama. But there was no drama. She heard what I had to said, took it in, and ended up doing it her own way anyway. She proved to me that she was right, but more important empowered me to have authentic conversations with her from there on.

Why do men brag about their accomplishments?

The quick answer is we brag for our own benefit, not for the benefit of others in the room. Men are gauged by what they are able to do, and when we brag we are really looking for internal inspiration to continue seeing ourselves as a champion who can deliver when asked. One thing that many men don't admit to is the more we brag the more insecure we are feeling. Men brag in a variety of ways, including talking about our memberships, homes, vacations, cars, contacts, and the like. There is always a small percentage of bullshit in our brag, but normally we are cautious not to go too far in case we get found out and look like chumps. Bragging is a part of our interaction with each other.

Why don't men show their emotions?

Because we are taught that it is weak to do so. Men don't cry! Or if we do, we'll rarely admit to it. The truth is we do get emotional; we just don't show it. Our fathers pull us aside and tell us to be two-faced—a private face you have outside of the public eye and a public face that shows no weakness.

Why do my male colleagues talk over me at meetings?

One of the most frustrating things to an Alpha Male is a meeting. That frustration is only surpassed by having to talk about details. When men talk over women and each other in meetings, what they are really saying is, "I'm frustrated and I don't want to be here. Your focus on details and not getting to the point is wasting my time!" They will try to rush through the meeting because they don't see the value of having a meeting longer than five minutes. Alpha Males are thinking, "Tell me what I need to know in 30 seconds and then let me out of here!"

Example A: The woman who gets talked over would say:

"I think talking about who we are going to choose as a supplier is important. We need to consider region, reach, reputation, pricing, and details around how we are going to formulate our agreement. Then we should decide how we are going to roll out the program, who will do what, how we will keep accountable, and what our milestones will be."

Example B: The woman who has the complete attention of the group would say:

"We can all agree that, at the end of the day, we will be leaders in manufacturing. In order to take and keep this place in the market, we need to make important decisions to ensure that we are successful at every step. These are the decisions we have to make that will make or break us: which suppliers we want to use, who we will choose to rise to the top with us, what agreement we'll have to make sure they deliver what they promise to us, and how we will roll out the program to make sure that we are all in the winner's circle as quickly as possibly. Shall we talk about the goal-related details now?"

If men are talking over you, they are frustrated and they want out of the meeting. Make it relevant, goal related, and based in success.

Why do men rush to decisions without considering all the details?

We are goal oriented. The rest is just white noise. We aim, ready, shoot. We watch cowboy movies as kids and see that they guy who draws his gun the quickest wins. The challenge with this, of course, is that we often miss (though we won't admit to it), but we also have the advantage of getting deals because we are the quickest to post. I believe that Alpha Males make the best decision possible with the information they have. As they get more information, they may change course, but they are not ones to wait around and see how things turn out.

Women, on the other hand, almost always hit it out of the ballpark—that is, if the game is in play by the time they come to their conclusions.

I've had clients who prepare, over prepare, and re-prepare for a prospective deal only to hear that it was already given to someone else. Remember, the big take from the small and the quick take from the big. If a guy sits there waiting for something to line up properly, he is seen as weak and loses the respect of other men in the room. You see it as rushing forward without all the details; we see it as taking action when someone needs to lead.

Getting Promoted: Taking Command of Your Own Ship

How do I overcome a feeling of powerlessness in my professional career?

Start to plan. Every woman should have a main plan and a Plan B. This is how men manage their careers. Our main plan is the path that we are following. Our expectations are built with dates in mind as well as milestones to let us know we are on the right track. Then we have a Plan B. This is if something goes haywire and we need to do a radical move.

Here is an example of what a main plan and a Plan B could look like for a female accountant.

Main Plan:

"I am going to work hard with my downtown firm and learn as much as I can about accounting. I am going to take extra courses, work on as many diverse files as I can, build a network of professionals who refer to me, treat my clients exceptionally, and look to form alliances with other professionals in financial services. After three years, I will have developed a strong clientele, and I want my yearly billings to be a ratio of 3:1 of my salary. By year five, I will approach the partners of my firm with a partnership proposal and look to take my career to the next level. Once I make partner, I will start my family, continue to build the practice, and take a two-month sabbatical every year to write my grandfather's biography."

Plan B:

"If things don't go well with my firm and I don't think there will be partnership potential there for me, I am going to start researching other firms that might be a better fit for me. The network I am going to build will be beneficial for this. At year three I will make a decision on what the next step will be. The way I see it, I have three main options: stay with this firm, move to another firm, or potentially start my own practice. The main focus is to develop clients and contacts so that I hedge my bets regardless of the outcome. I will also start to study small business so that I'll know what I'm doing if I do start my own firm."

How do I ask my boss to give me more responsibility?

The first thing to do is ask yourself if you have been successful in previous responsibilities and have shown a capacity to get work done. Then ask yourself if you can handle additional workload to what you already have. If this all looks good, make an appointment with your boss and tell him you want to take on more.

Example:

"Bob, I'm excited about the work I've been responsible for this year and have all the projects in control, on budget, and on timetable. I'm interested in challenging myself and would like to take on more responsibility. What are some of the projects that I can get involved with to take my performance up to the next level?"

Notice that you first let him know that you have been successful with everything you have been responsible for (showing your ability to perform). That you have a willingness to continue to achieve (this shows you're goal oriented). Then you ask him an open-ended question to let him know that you want some feedback now and don't want him just to get back to you. If you want it, don't take no for an answer. He may try to blow you off to see if you are serious. Alpha Males love people who go the distance to get what they want.

Why do men make partner quicker than women?

This is the simple and controversial answer: Men are better at bringing in deals in most professional settings. Although women generally possess more advanced skills that are necessary for putting deals together, they often take a secondary position to a dominant male. Men are goal oriented, and at the end of the day the person who brings in the deal has the control. My dad refers to this as the difference between men's and women's definitions of the "golden rule." Women define it as "Treat others as you'd like them to treat you." Men's definition of the rule is "He who has the gold makes the rules."

To be completely blunt, you are made partner for one of two reasons: you are a major profit generator for the firm and your leaving would have a negative impact on the company's bottom line, or you are a strong ambassador for the company and your leaving would have a negative effect.

As men, we are taught that being a support person is being someone's slave. You are either at the top of the food chain, or you are waiting for someone else to fill your soup can. A man who can't make partner is a pile-on to other men. We know this, thus we try to put enormous deals together to solidify our earning a place at the table. Women think that being a good clutch player who supports the team's initiatives should have proved their commitment and thus they should be offered partnership as a reward.

Here is a quick equation to determine if you should be considered for partnership:

Take your annual salary. Add any assistants or support staff that work on your files. Then take into account the cost of you doing business (office space, computers, phones, company cars, etc.). Add all of these items up and then subtract that number from your billings/profit generation for the company. You will see what's left over. Decide if you think that number is worth having a share of the profits.

One client I worked with is a lawyer with a large firm in New York City. She had been at the same firm for 12 years and hadn't been offered partnership. She watched male counterparts being offered partnership after six years. We looked at her numbers and this is what they looked like:

Her salary	**$160,000**
Her assistant's salary	**$60,000**
Her office costs (approximately)	**$12,000**
Her expenses (expense account/car/travel)	**$25,000**
Her billings	**$360,000**
Profit to company	**$103,000**

She made her firm **$103,000** per year, or $8,583 per month, which may seem like a lot to you and me, but her profitability was just 29 **percent** of her billings.

In business, we like to have employees generate three times their salaries in billable time. That means for her to fit into this equation she would have to generate $480,000 in billable time. She was deficient by $120,000 per year. It wasn't that she wasn't working hard. It was just that, from a man's point of view, there would be no reason for her to also get a share of the firm's profits as a partner by billing so little. One other thing to consider is she had done an exceptional job at servicing clients, but had not brought in a single client in 12 years. She had kept busy getting files from partners and colleagues. Let me give you an example of a partner's numbers:

His salary	**$600,000**
His assistants' salaries (3)	**$180,000**
His office costs (approximately)	**$30,000**

His expenses (expense account/car/travel)	**$120,000**
His billings	**$2,600,000**
Profit to company	**$1,643,000**

It's obvious that his salary is almost four times hers and his expenses are exponentially larger. That's because he is spending a lot of time bringing in new clients, building networks, and developing relationships that bring in more and more work. His billings are related to the work he is bringing in and then handing off to associates like my client. His profitability is 63 percent, or double hers. If he were to leave with those clients, it would have a noticeable financial impact on the firm. Unlike her $8,583 in profit generation per month, he was generating $136,916 per month in profit. He was earning the company almost 15 times the amount of money that she was. If she were generating money for the firm like that, she would be a partner.

Regardless of whether your firm is full of chauvinists on the partner level, if you can bring your profitability (billable time) up to a point where the firm begins to feel the effect of your efforts, you too will be offered partnership for one of two reasons: They appreciate that you are a hunter and can bring in work, or they are worried that you'll take all your new clients and open up your own shop. Either way, the power is yours.

Why am I always training my subordinates to become my superiors?

You have been identified as a clutch hitter (read: support player), and men are exceptional at finding people to help us build what we want built and maximizing that person's contribution. The first question I have is, have you applied for senior positions or are you waiting for them to notice you and ask you to apply? If you haven't applied, what are you waiting for? If you have applied and are getting passed over, there may be a couple of reasons for this:

- You have been deep-sixed.
- There is no worry from the powers above that you will leave.
- They have assessed the risk that you will leave, and they aren't worried about it. You have not been positioned as a player and thus are not under consideration.
- If they have a good trainer (who are hard to find and we don't know how to do it), why would they promote you unless they had to? If they do, they have to find someone who can do your job as well as you did, which means more work for us. We aren't overly excited about taking on extra work.

An easy way to rectify this, if you are sure you haven't been deep-sixed, is to sit down with your superiors and ask them what it would take for you to be promoted. Then tell them that you want to follow their prescription as well as put into place a system for training that you use so that, when promoted, you can train your replacement.

Now here is the important thing: Do not give them this system until you have been promoted. If they are looking for a reason to turf you, you're providing them with a system that may be their only reason to keep you on. If you think this to be the case, start working on your Plan B.

What does it take for a woman to be considered an equal in business?

The first thing is to respect yourself and only allow people to interact with you if they are respectful. The second thing is to become a deal maker. Look to put together deals for your firm that showcase your ability to generate business. None of us is born with this talent (although I can't think of an Alpha Male who would agree with me), so look for mentors to share the process of putting deals together. The third thing is to act professionally. If you want to be a winner, act like a winner. The fourth thing is be careful with whom you spend time. My dad says, "If you want to fly with eagles, don't run with turkeys." You will acquire the characteristics of the people you spend time with.

Remember how men define the golden rule. At the end of the day, you will be judged on your ability to be successful in your profession. The fifth thing I can state is winners do what losers won't. As an Alpha Male, I want to spend time with colleagues (regardless of gender) who can get the job done.

Family versus Career or Family with Career: With or without a Crew

Will it negatively affect me if I don't work weekends?

I think working weekends if overrated unless you are building your own business. There is no reason why you can't get your work done during the week. There will be occasions when you have to see a client on a weekend or come in to close a deal, but generally men won't be impressed that you are in on the weekends; we'll think that you are inefficient and have to come in on the weekends to catch up.

Why do women have to choose between having a successful career and having a family?

In the past, women have been forced (through public pressure) to choose career or choose family. If they tried to do both, they would either be bad mothers or they wouldn't be able to fulfill responsibilities at home. Things are different now.

Women have more resources available to them to support their transition, and public opinion now honors a woman who has it all. When you make the decision that you want to have both, and not at the expense of each other, you can have both.

I think that the biggest mistake I see women make is doing both without a plan in place. Female friends of mine say, "I think we are going to start a family." I ask them, "What are you going to do about your work?" The consistent response is, "I'll just go on maternity leave and pick it up when I come back."

This is a huge mistake. They are giving up their power over the situation and deciding that they will just wait to see what happens. Are you kidding me? I suggest to the women in my life that they plan for how they can keep their career going while they are pregnant and after they have their kids. One does not have to go on pause for the other.

A friend of mine is an accountant and one day when I was talking to her about her pregnancy, she said that she was starting to slow down because she would be going on leave in the next few months so there was no point bringing in new files. It was April when we were having the discussion and she had just finished a busy tax season.

I told her that she was crazy. Now was the time to be bringing in files. She could build the relationship before she left and be back in time to do their tax planning the following year. I could see in her eyes that she hadn't considered that yet. Then I told her to have a look at the playgroup she was a part of where there were 30 women in the group. I asked her, "What do the women do that are in your group?" She replied, "I'm not sure, I think they are just moms." I said to her, "What do they think you do?" She said, "I think they probably think that I'm just a mom."

As it turns out, under closer investigation, there were three chief financial officers, a North American director of sales, three lawyers, and a well-known food manufacturing company owner.

All of these women were a touch gloomy because they felt out of the circle of business. Once they realized they had something in common other than their kids, they started to discuss how they could do business together when they were back. My friend returned to her position after seven months with $325,000 in new files from her new mom contacts. Don't look at having a family as a time out from business. Look at the opportunities that can be created in your new position as a mom.

Am I going to negatively affect my position in my company if I go on maternity leave?

Yes and no. How it will affect you depends on how you deal with it. After waiting for the first trimester, most women tell their boss they are pregnant and what their approximate due date is. Then they tell the boss how much time they will be taking off and leave.

When you do this to your boss, you are basically saying, "I'm pregnant. I'll be leaving in four months. You need to figure out what you are going to do with my responsibilities while I'm gone. Find someone who is willing to come in for my maternity leave. Then you are going to need to train them on how to do my job. Then you have to hope that they don't leave while I'm gone to take a full-time job somewhere else. If that happens, you'll have to find another temp to train." And so on. The pregnancy just became another thing on the boss's desk to deal with. Is it any wonder the boss isn't happy? This is why a friend's boss responded with "Congratulations. Shit. Shit. Shit." This is why men don't look forward to female staff going on maternity leave. It creates a lot of work for us.

My recommendation is to have a plan prepared for your boss to cover your leave. Let me share with you what one client did when she decided to tell her boss. After her first trimester, she forecasted the dates she would be gone from work with her pediatrician and her husband. Then she booked an appointment with her boss at her accounting firm to sit down with him to discuss her pregnancy.

She told him that she would be leaving in four months to go on maternity leave (unless some complication came up where she would have to leave earlier). She said that she had a colleague in mind who she would start briefing on her files and what needed to get done for each client. Before she left, she would be available to this person should any questions arise around a file. Then after having her baby, she was planning to return to work slowly after four months.

She would start by coming in one day a week and have files at home that she would work on when her energy allowed her to. She planned to buy a laptop for her house, and had talked to the IT department regarding loading software on her laptop and setting up a connection so that she could get office files through the Internet. She would let her clients know that she was leaving and introduce them to the person who would be covering her files. If at any time a client wanted to talk directly to her, she would be checking e-mail twice a week and voicemail at least once. As well, her replacement could call her at home between 9 AM and 4 PM Monday through Friday.

Her boss looked at her and said, "Thank you and congratulations!" She came up with a customized plan so that she didn't drop the ball on her responsibilities and didn't add more work to his plate. She had devised a solution, and although she wouldn't be there physically she would still be available should issues arise. If more women did this, there wouldn't be so much negativity around maternity leave. You can't relinquish your professional responsibilities when you are pregnant and still be taken seriously by your peers. If you take the time to formulate a plan, you can enjoy your pregnancy and your career without putting either one in jeopardy.

When is the best time for me to start a family?

I think the best time for you to start a family and keep your career on track is when you have proven that you are profitable. When you start bringing in clients, closing big deals, or forming big alliances for your firm, it is the most opportune time for you to start working on a family. Your value to your firm will be at its highest when you have showcased your ability to close. If you take time off to start your family and you are just pushing paper, everyone is going to see you as working the system and being a cost on the firm.

If you have brought in work, the perception changes and people will say, "She's taking time off, but she deserves it. She just brought in that big file."

Don't be of the mindset that you are going to start your family and then take your career seriously when your kids are in school. It won't work out that way. If you start shaking it up after you have kids, your colleagues will always worry that your family will get in the way of your closing deals. Give yourself a taste of being a deal closer and showcase to the rest of your firm that you can deliver. The question of whether you can close will become moot. You want to be seen as a closer who has a family, and not as a mom who carefully manages balance between professional commitments and family responsibilities. Even though this will be a balancing act that you will master, it isn't anyone's business how you manage it. All they need to know is that you can deliver.

Is it okay to talk about family if a coworker brings it up?

I don't. Although I share stories about Jacqui (with her permission), I can count on one hand how many times I've had a colleague or client over to my house. I am a strong believer in keeping my private life private. I don't share with people when my birthday is, when my anniversary is, when a family member has been sick, and so on. I make two assumptions:

1. Nobody cares about my life except me.
2. It's nobody's business but mine.

I find that female clients and colleagues tell me everything about their life, their friends, their background, their relationships, and so on. I need to know this about clients I'm coaching, but I'm often shocked how much colleagues tell me about their personal lives.

I had an assistant working with me in Kamloops, and I knew everything about her life: who she was dating, highlights from her high school years, her best friends, her best friends' relationships, everything. I called her on it one day and asked her, "Why do you tell everyone all your personal details?" She said, "So do you!"

So I quizzed her. "How long have I been with Jacqui?" "What's my dad's name?" "When's my birthday?" She just looked at me. Then I said, "Your last four boyfriends were Ted, John, Ben, and Josh. Your dad's name is Kevin. Your birthday is July 18th."

Because women are exceptional communicators, they like to converse with others. When men experience this, the challenge is two fold. The first is we are taught to play our cards somewhat close to our chest and not to give any more information than is absolutely necessary. The second thing is men don't understand why you would talk about personal things when you should be talking about business things. These are the two reactions that we will share with you, but here is a third one we don't bring up: The more you tell us the harder it will be to make decisions that might be good for business, which is bad for you.

We need to be objective when making business decisions, and we want people to be objective when making decisions about us. I would rather be fired than have someone say, "Let Chris stay. He has a family." Every man wants to be in the deal because he deserves it, not because someone felt sorry for him.

Without being cold, try to steer away from sharing personal information if you don't have to. Other people can tell you anything they want, but play your cards close to your chest.

Office Relationships: Sailing off Course

Do I have to go out for drinks after work, and, if so, how many should I have?

My strongest suggestion for you is that you do not have to go out every time people meet after work, but you should go some of the time. If male counterparts invite you out for drinks in the group, it means that they are looking to bring you within an inner level of intimacy.

Men have a couple of rules when it comes to drinking. First, we only drink with people we like. Second, we are always looking for ways not to pay. Third, if we are inviting you out for drinks, we want to test you to see if you can fit into the group and to see how you act in a social setting. Being invited is almost always a positive, but you don't want to make it a habit.

Groups of men often go out for drinks after a big deal, on Fridays to welcome the weekend, to celebrate someone's birthday, or because things are rough and they are looking to let some steam off.

My recommendation is, go out for deal celebrations and to let off some steam. Forget the Friday watering hole tradition, and when it is someone's birthday just do a 15-minute cameo appearance and then take off.

When you are having drinks with the group, the rule is no more than two drinks. Add one drink if you have a strong constitution, and have one less if you can't hold your alcohol. Nothing will destroy you quicker than being a lush and having your male colleagues see you, even if they are sloshed as well. You do not want to become a corporate legend around the water cooler. I've seen many careers destroyed like this, and the women never even knew it had an effect.

Now stopping at one, two, or three drinks can be difficult, especially due to peer pressure. My trick (I never have more that three drinks in 24 hours and I'm 280 lbs!) is to excuse myself after the first round, find the server, and tell him or her that I'm not drinking any more, but to deliver me non-alcoholic beverages that look like what I was drinking before and that they are free to charge me the same price as the alcoholic beverage. This is not deceitful, lying, or anything negative. Instead it allows you keep your power in a business setting without looking like a prude to the group.

If I think a colleague is being treated unfairly, how should I intervene?

I think that there are certain times when you have to step in, especially if someone's human rights are being violated. However, when you step in, make sure that you are prepared to go the distance. You can't kind of step in. You either do or you don't. If you do step in, do not back down! You have to go all in.

I have watched colleagues jump to someone's aid when they think something is unjust. They usually end up being targeted as well, and are taken down with the person they are trying to help. In most cases the situation doesn't require someone to get involved. If someone is getting in trouble because they didn't do something, you shouldn't get involved. If someone is getting chastised for his actions, you shouldn't get involved. If someone is being mentally, physically, or emotionally abused, you should intervene without putting yourself in danger. Bring a member of your HR department into the circle and ask that your involvement (in letting them know) be kept in confidence. In the event that there is no HR department, pull the person being abused aside and offer them options. Let your integrity be your guide, but don't save someone just to save him. Get involved only if they can't defend themselves and the treatment isn't deserved.

What role does office politics play in professional success?

Office politics is a black vortex in business. It is a strong influencing factor on what happens in a business setting. The mistake people make is getting involved in the politics. I believe that it is important to know what is going on, but you don't need to be involved in order to do this. Think of yourself as an observer, rather than a participant, and you should be fine. Remember, for one group to win in office politics another must lose. I just don't like the odds.

What should I do if I'm forced to take sides on an issue at work?

This plays into the discussion about office politics. Everyone involved will want to know where you stand, and if you take sides you are going to please one group and piss off the other. I think this is the perfect time to take the higher ground and stay out of it. If you say to the group, "I'd rather not get involved," you are going to look like a weak fence-sitter who doesn't take a stand on issues.

Instead, my strategy has always been to say, "While all of you are fighting over who is right and who is wrong, I'm going to focus on the project so this little rift doesn't sink all of us." You are letting them know that they are acting like kids and you, while not directly chastising them, are not going to take your focus off the work that needs to be done.

What should I do if I'm attracted to a coworker?

Men learn a lesson early in our careers: Do not dip your pen in the company ink. This is a crude way of illustrating a point. Office romances rarely work out, and the woman always faces the brunt of the jokes.

We worked with a city mayor who decided to hit on a secretary who intimated she was interested in him. They had a relationship, and she went from being a receptionist to being a business development officer in a few short months. He said that he moved her into that position because she was bright and talented and he knew she would do the job well. Having met her, I can tell you that he was correct.

But, from that day on, she was the object of ridicule by all her associates and people in other cities. She wasn't the business development officer for this city; she was the mayor's concubine who got a job to keep her out of trouble and so that he could keep an eye on her. Her professional life at that point ceased to have any currency. They ended the relationship, and she left the city.

She applied to well over 100 municipalities for work, but because she was known as the slut who slept her way into her position she couldn't even get an interview. The saddest part of this story is that it was nobody's business they had a relationship, and she was very good at her job as a business development officer. Yet all people remember is that she slept with the mayor. The last I heard, she moved to the other side of the country to look for work.

Because women have historically used sexuality in business, women who have relationships in the workplace are thought to be unskilled and thus must use other means to show their value. Women don't need this extra challenge in their career. There are a lot of great people out there. Look outside your office and even outside your industry to find someone who won't conflict with your profession and won't call into question your abilities as a professional.

If a colleague is having personal problems, how can I respectfully offer my help?

Don't. It isn't any of your business. If you get involved in their personal lives, you will not be able to interact with them objectively and professionally. Do not cross the line! And when in doubt, mind your own business. You don't need to have friends at work. Have your friends after work and on weekends. Women screw up business relationships by trying to be buddy-buddy with coworkers. I'm not saying that you can't like them or them you, but these people should have no vested interest in your life and vice versa. Keep them separate.

I'm already in a relationship with someone in my office. How should I deal with it?

If it isn't serious yet, break it off. If it is serious, one of you should consider leaving the company and taking another position. You may think this extreme, but the relationship you are in will have a major effect on your reputation. He will feel the effect as well, but you will take the brunt of it. If you can, get out and swear him to secrecy. If he is your boss, end it now (people will think you are sleeping your way to the top). If he is a subordinate, end it now (people will think you are misusing your power). This is trouble.

If you disagree with me and think that everything will be fine, I want you to dog ear this page and come back to it in a month. You will see things differently. Trust me, a workplace romance is a kiss of death.

Should I invite my boss or colleagues over to my house for dinner?

I don't think that you should ever cross the line between your professional relationships and your personal geography. If you want to have a supper meeting to discuss business, take them out for dinner at their favorite restaurant. I have had bosses who have said, "Oh, I'd love to meet Jacqui. All of us should have dinner." I smiled and said, "That would be nice," but I knew that it would never happen.

There is no upside to having him or her at my house, but there are downsides. The less your contacts know about your personal life, the better. If you are self employed, I support having clients over for supper or to your weekend cabin, but even then the lines can become foggy between friendship and business. Only invite professional contacts into your personal space if you have an intention behind it and you are prepared for a negative outcome. Play it safe and meet on neutral ground.

Should I invite a colleague out for my birthday?

I wouldn't. Try to keep your personal and professional lives separate, especially if there is alcohol involved. I'd suggest keeping your birthday to yourself and keeping the festivities to personal contacts. Again, your business associates should be kept separate from your personal friends.

Should I give my boss a Christmas gift?

Not unless you got a promotion or a fat Christmas bonus. If you did, give him a bottle of 15-year-old Scotch. This always hits the spot unless he's an alcoholic. Then you are in trouble. If you give a gift just to give a gift, you look like an ass-kisser. Everyone hates an ass-kisser, even the boss. If you make the company money or bring in opportunities, that's gift enough because he will be taking credit for it behind closed doors.

Why do women get catty with each other in business?

I think women go after each other because they are trying to get on the guys' team. What they fail to realize is there are not a limited amount of spaces in getting into business with men. If you can deliver, you can have a space. Women seem to think that they need to eliminate each other to play with the big boys and go after people. But there is nothing honorable about taking a run at a female colleague, and we don't think it is impressive, especially when women go head-to-head with each other for everyone to see.

A great example of women gutting each other was on the series, *The Apprentice*. In the first season, they split the teams between men and women. The women were destroying the men in competition week after week (because they focused on process). They were all laughing and celebrating and enjoying the fruits of their collective efforts.

Then, because so many men had been let go, the show was forced to restructure the teams. All of a sudden the sisterhood of the women was out the window, and they were now working hard at getting the men to accept them. They started verbally attacking each other, and the men just got out of the way and let them kill each other off. The last two contestants were both men.

The greatest enemy to women in business is women. Men know this and methodically step out of the way and let them catfight. Women who go after each other do a huge disservice to women in business and undermine their integrity and reputation in business. Remember, you are not competing for that last seat at the table. If you can deliver, they'll find a chair for you.

Emotional Management: Incoming Tide

What should I do if I feel like I'm going to start to cry?

The first thing to do is to excuse yourself and go to the washroom. If you need to cry, cry. Sharing your emotions in a business setting isn't wrong, but depending on the situation some people will think that you don't have control. Men have a default when women excuse themselves. We think it is a "woman issue" and act like it never happened. If the tears do start, do not make excuses! You don't have to explain anything to anybody. Just say that you need to be excused and will be back shortly.

I have seen men so irate in meetings that they are on the verge of tears. The reason that emotions get so overwhelming in almost every case (men and women) is that they are taking something personally. If you feel like the tears might come on, take a mental step back and think to yourself, "In the overall picture of my career is this a deal breaker?" If it is, then excuse yourself and let the tears flow.

My guess is it is an event that has strong emotion tied to it at the moment, but in the overall picture it is minute. And repeat after me: Do not take the situation personally! It isn't personal; it is business. And if you do cry, it's spilt milk. Don't get stuck on it. It happens, so move on!

What are some of the fears men have in business?

I think that men have as many, if not more, fears than women in business. Here are the 12 most common fears we have, but won't admit to:

1. Being considered a weak link
2. Peers thinking that we can't do our job
3. Being considered a fraud
4. Disappointing our mentors
5. Being poor
6. Getting fired
7. Being considered a bully or a man who commits sexual harassment
8. Embarrassing our fathers and spouses
9. Not having control over the outcome
10. People making jokes behind our back
11. Others finding out that sometimes we fake our confidence
12. Wasting our time on things that won't matter (we want to do work that people will remember and talk about in the future)

Navigating the Waters of Political Correctness

Is it okay to let a man open a door for me in a professional setting?

Yes, yes, yes. You are not giving up your power by allowing a man to be a gentleman. With the mainstreaming of feminism in the last few decades, men find themselves in a climate where we are unsure if we should practice all those manners that our mothers drilled into us. If a man wants to open the door for you, pull out your chair, or walk on the curbside when you both walk down the street, let him. He'll make his mother proud and reinforce to him that you are deserving of a certain level of respect.

Should I explain my position in the firm if a male client assumes I'm a secretary?

Do this without making him wrong. Men make assumptions that we regret, so allow us to slither out gracefully and we'll thank you for it. Many of my female clients will walk into a room with a bunch of men who will assume she is a secretary or a paralegal.

One way to avoid this is to introduce yourself immediately and include your position. "Hi, welcome to Flett, Wilkie, and Finnie. My name is Lisa MacKay, and I am a senior litigator with the commercial group." This will quickly position you in the room as a lawyer.

If the mistake has already occurred, quickly correct it.

Man: "Excuse me. Could you please get me a cup of coffee?"

You: "No problem, let me get one of my assistants in here and he'll get it for you right away."

You are giving him a way to save face without letting him know that he made a mistake. It is classy and will hold a lot of weight with him.

What should I do if male colleagues treat me like a secretary?

Call an assistant and delegate it out. Say, "Jon needs some support. Would you please take care of it for him?" The worst thing you can do is to play the role and go do it. It is a good way to put your boundary in place that you aren't a pile-on for his work and let him know that you are an equal to him. Next time, he'll call a support staff. Some men will do this just to see what you'll do. Don't play into it.

When out with mixed company, who should pick up the check?

It all depends on the situation. Here is how I go through the process of deciding who should pay: The person who made the invitation, the person who stands to benefit the greatest from the meeting, the most senior position at the table.

If you are just out with colleagues to have lunch during a planning session, throw in for your own lunch. If it is business related and you benefit from having them eat with you (i.e., you are brainstorming an idea, collecting information, assessing opportunities, or delegating work), pick up the check. When it doubt, take care of the bill. Nobody likes a cheapskate!

If you are out with a client who always grabs the bill or with your boss who does the same, excuse yourself to the restroom and give your credit card to the waiter. Then when you come back from the restroom, sign your tab and go back to the table. When people are ready to pay and your boss/client is looking for the check, tell them that you have already taken care of it and it was a pleasure to share a meal with them. They will be impressed that you took care of it without their knowing.

Manhandling: Avoiding Shark Bites

What should I do if a man starts to raise his voice in a meeting?

The best strategy here is to drop the volume of your voice when you talk to him. When men are getting rattled and looking for verbal combat, they need to hear what you are saying so they can attack it. As you drop the volume of your voice, he is forced not to speak as loud so that he can hear you.

When he sees that he is yelling or talking quite loudly, he will be concerned that people in the meeting are seeing him get overly emotional, and that isn't something a man wants to be known for. I don't suggest you talk like you are scared or intimidated. Just talk at the volume you would in a library. As he starts to come down, you can increase your volume back to normal. This is a great trick, and I've seen it in action. It works amazingly well.

How should I deal with a man who says something offensive?

The first thing is to not laugh or make light of it. Give him a look that says, "Please tell me you didn't say what I think you just said." After he says his offensive statement, tell him that you'd like to talk privately to him after the meeting or (if outside a meeting) as soon as possible.

When you say this to him, he will revert to being the four-year-old who, after acting up in the store, has been told by his mother that they need to have a discussion when they get to the car. If you bring it up in mixed company, you will embarrass him and he will look to deep-six you.

Instead, in private, tell him that his comment could be considered offensive and that you wanted to share with him that certain comments might be contrived differently by mixed company. Do not make him wrong! Instead, present the information as if you are trying to give him the woman's point of view on the situation. Men often say things without thinking of the repercussions to the opposite sex. Because it isn't a big deal with men, we assume it isn't a big deal with everyone.

I remember at one speaking engagement I said to the group, "As a rule of thumb, you will want to. ..." I continued on with my speech and, at the end, an older woman pulled me aside and said, "I wanted to share something with you that I heard you say in your presentation. You referred to a 'rule of thumb.' That refers to an old law where men could beat their wives with a piece of wood no thicker than their thumb. I know that isn't what you meant, and most members of your audience may not be familiar with that saying, but I wanted to share that with you as a small gift from me to you."

I can tell you that I was shocked and appreciative at the same time. I hadn't considered where the saying came from, and I now consciously don't use that saying given that I know its origin and the effect it could have on some audience members.

One thing to remember is to not let these comments go by without being dealt with. You have a responsibility to male colleagues and, more important, to your female colleagues to ensure that language in a business setting is always positive, supportive, and not offensive. If you let these comments go, you are doing as much a disservice as the person making them.

What should I say if a man says something offensive directly to me?

Let him know that you need to have a talk in private directly after the situation. When face to face with him, tell him that he is never to talk to you like that again and then leave. Do not explain yourself; do not talk about why it was offensive. Simply let him know that he has crossed a boundary with you and that it is unacceptable.

You are not saying that what he said is wrong; you are saying that what he said is unacceptable to you. If you suggest why it was offensive to you, you open yourself up to debate on whether you are being too sensitive, taking it wrong, misunderstanding the comment, and so on. Do not open it up for conversation. Let him know the line has been crossed and it won't be tolerated.

I had a client in San Francisco who was working within a male-dominated industry. She was in a senior level position, and her boss, who was a hothead, said to her after a tirade, "I didn't mean to get so mad, it's just sometimes you remind me of my wife when you don't listen." She was shocked that he would say that, and after a few minutes, when she removed the emotion from the situation, she called him and told him that they needed to have a word in private. The first thing he said was, "Why, what's wrong?" She went into his office and said, "You are never to talk to me like that again. It crossed a boundary, and I'm not okay with that." Then she walked out and back to her desk. She has not had an issue with him since. You do not have to make him wrong to ensure your boundaries are respected.

What should I do if a man begins to act aggressively?

You should collect your things, tell him that the situation is not achieving any goals and you'd like to give him some space to consider his position, and then leave.

One thing that scares the hell out of dominant Alpha Males is that we are seen as bullies to women and get a reputation for acting inappropriately. Reputation is key to us, and most of us want to be seen as sharks focused on the relentless drive towards success. None of us wants to be seen as a man who uses intimidation to get what he wants. As long as you stay there, you are giving him an outlet to act up.

By letting him know that you won't be party to this type of situation, you let him know that he crossed your boundaries and acted in a way that is unacceptable to you. You don't have to spell out that his aggression is the reason you are leaving, you can go back to the goal language by suggesting that the goal will not be reached at this meeting. He can't fight if you aren't there.

The worse thing you can do is to try to go toe to toe with him. If you lose, he'll think you are weak. If you win, he'll look to deep-six you. If you leave, you are controlling the environment, not the situation that he is trying to dominate.

What is the best way to remind a guy about the professional promises he has made?

Men agree to do a lot of things in the moment, but we are kings of procrastination. We are so busy looking for goals to tackle that we often forget about the promises we have made to others. This happens almost entirely with women, because a man asking other man for a favor isn't as frequent. When we do ask each other for favors, it is normally a big one. The simplest way to get a man to do what he promises is to remind him of what he agreed to do and, if you can, prep anything that he needs to do it. For example:

A male colleague has agreed to write a promotion on your behalf. The deadline is coming up, and you still haven't received anything from him. Rather than getting mad at him for not honoring his commitment, drop him an e-mail that says something like this:

> *Hi Chris, hope things are well. I really appreciate you saying that you will write that endorsement for me regarding the promotion to brand manager. I know that your schedule is extremely busy and time is a premium. Because the deadline is this Friday to get my application in and I want you included in it, would you mind if I prepped a letter for you to review, rather than writing from scratch? That way, I can get exactly what I need it to say, you can make sure that it is what you want to say, and it will take you a fraction of the time. Let me*

know if this fits and I'll have something off to you by this afternoon.
Cheers,
Anne

You have reminded him that his promise to you is important, you have identified the goal (have it in by Friday), and you have offered to get it started (so he doesn't have to do the details work). This is the best way to go about having him fulfill his promises.

If you choose to tell him that he hasn't fulfilled his commitment and you want him to keep his word, prepare to get deep-sixed. Our word is our bond, and we are all brought up to keep our word. Although you see this as him breaking his word, he will have told himself that it was a small oversight about an unimportant thing. These are little lies we tell ourselves to preserve our honor. Bring his word into question and he'll be gunning for you.

If I want to make a suggestion to a male colleague about how he could do something better, how should I bring it up?

My first suggestion is ... don't. When you give a suggestion, he'll take it as a criticism and most likely will start silently gunning for you. If, however, the outcome of his actions affects you (i.e., a team goal, bonuses, etc.), you have two options: (1) start developing an alternative strategy that you can deploy when the project gets to the point of no return, or (2) make suggestions on how the team can support the leader to make his job easier (taking responsibility away with him with his consent as compared to taking it away from him).

Here is how you implement the first one.

Consider what the goal is and work backwards to develop your strategy. Look at how the project is going and what you think is wrong with what your male colleague is doing. What would you do differently? For what reasons do you think that the project is off track? Is it a bad presentation? Is the wrong person pitching the client? Are you offering the wrong product or service? What challenge is going to be faced by following the path that has been planned? What would you do differently? If you are confident with your prescribed course of action, start developing it.

Build your collateral, your strategy, and your deployment plan. Then look for an opportunity to share it with the team. Don't say, "I'm not too comfortable with where we were going so I've developed a new strategy." This will piss of all the men and make them gun for you because it is embarrassing to the guy taking the lead.

Instead, I'd suggest saying, "I've been doing a lot of research to really get familiar with this project, and I've been playing with some ideas around how we can ensure we'll close this deal (goal statement). I think we have a great foundation in place, and I'd like to share some additional strategies if everyone is up to it."

Now here is the moment of truth. If the rest of the group agrees that the train is off the rails, they will want to explore your ideas with vigor. If, however, everyone thinks that things are fine, offer your strategies to the guy in charge of the project and your immediate supervisor. Then you have documented a change of course, and if the project fails, you will be seen as the mine canary who saw the danger before the rest.

Now, if the second suggestion sounds better for you, here is how to deploy it.

Say to the team when they are convened, "I am excited where we are going with this project. I think Bob is doing a great job at managing this account. I'd be very interested in taking on more responsibility for the project to take some of the weight off him so that he can focus on the bigger stuff. Let's explore ways that each of us can dig in and support the project to ensure we hit our mark. Bob, where can the team give you a hand?" Now, if you have assessed where the challenges are, suggest those areas to offer more of a hand.

Here is the kicker: Do not discuss this strategy with anyone. Let me repeat: Do not share this strategy with anyone! If it is a conspiracy, it will come out sooner or later, and if that guy is still around, he will feel like a fool and will be looking for professional vengeance. The harshest part is you will never see it coming. You'll be deep-sixed and might not know it for years. If you bring this up with other coworkers, it becomes mutiny and men will see it as dishonest and disloyal. Even guys on side with you will not trust you for fear that you will do the same to them.

Hostile Takeovers and General Hostilities: Battleships

Why do male counterparts take credit for my work?

If male counterparts are taking credit for your work, it is a sure sign that they are totally insecure about their abilities in business. Strong men love to talk about the people they do business with; weak men look at where they can take credit for others because they know they aren't making the contribution that they should be or that people will expect from them.

When a male colleague does take credit for my work, what should I do?

The first thing is to keep your cool. You have just been placed into a very strong position. He knows that you know that he is full of shit. Now he has also taken credit for something he doesn't know how to do. If you play your cards right, you have him on the ropes. If you launch into an attack for the credit in front of peers, you will be considered dangerous and will become priority No. 1 on every man's deep-six list.

I recommend a more strategic and beneficial direction when you find yourself in this situation. You have two options. The first option is to deep-six him by asking him questions in a curious tone (not judgmental) about the details of how he developed the strategy. "Bob, could you give me a little more background on how you landed that account and the steps that led to your success?"

As he doesn't have the information, he will fumble, and the people in the group will see that he is full of it and call his credibility into question. By doing this, you have drawn a line in the sand, and he will know that you are gunning for him because the two of you are the only ones who have all the details. Only do this if you are prepared to go the distance.

Your second option, and the one I recommend, is to sit back and find an opportunity to connect with him. If he has taken credit for a component of a larger project, you have just become very valuable to him as he needs you now to achieve the next piece. Meet with him and say, "I'm really pleased at how this project has gone thus far, but I'm unsure if my involvement is furthering my career. I'm wondering if I should start to focus on other projects where my leadership skills can really shine through. I'd appreciate your opinion on this." This is you letting him know that you are about to step away from the project right at the most volatile time to let him lead, as it seemed he enjoyed telling everyone about his abilities.

Now he has one of two options: agree with you and let you move onto something else while he tries to find someone else to poach, or he will bring you to the forefront in other people's eyes to ensure that you will receive enough recognition to keep you in play. If you leave and the project crumbles, people will know that you were the real leader. If he starts to promote your abilities to peers, you are getting the recognition you deserve. Either way, you win.

What do I do if a male colleague scoops a client away from me?

Alpha Male response: Take care of your clients and they won't be taken away. If your clients are being taken by a male colleague, you probably haven't let your clients know that you are their contact, you have allowed your colleague to do work that you should have done, you haven't instilled confidence in your client where they trust you and feel like you have their trust, or simply stated the guy is a slime ball. Alpha Males like taking what we want because we get kicks out of deciding to take something and then acquiring it.

From a professional point, it is important that the client never knows there is conflict. I would have a meeting with your colleague and ask what happened. When he plays stupid (which he undoubtedly will), I would say, "Listen, you and I are playing on the same team. Let's agree to respect each other's client list so that we can focus on bringing new clients in, instead of poaching clients from each other. I know that this wasn't your intention, so I wanted to agree to some ground rules. Let's agree that when we have a client, it stays our client. What are your thoughts?"

You aren't blaming him, but you are letting him know that you know he poached those clients and, unless he wants to spend all his time guarding his clients from you, he best consider himself warned. This is strong, respectful, and lets him know that you aren't a pushover. But let me go back to the obvious. When a client comes in, tell them that you are going to be their go-to person and, regardless of who works on the file, the buck stops here. Let your clients know that you will be looking out for their best interest and they will start a relationship built on trust with you.

What do I do if a colleague declares war on me?

Pull them aside privately as soon as possible and say, "I understand there is friction between us. I want to get to the bottom of it so that any issue we may have won't get in the way of us being successful. Let's discuss the issue and look for ways we can deal with it discretely and without making fools of ourselves."

When you put it this way, you are going to remind the person that going at each other is unprofessional and, if it continues, they are going to look ridiculous to everyone else. If they share their challenge with you, seek to first understand and then to be understood. Don't leave the meeting until things are cleared up. If the individual doesn't have anything to say, consider the issue closed. If anything else comes up around it, prepare for battle and deep-six them. If you have warned them and they still decide to go at you, take them out.

I had a colleague, Bill, who I was working with a few years ago and I decided not to pull him in on a deal I was working on. He got pissed and decided to tell people that I was not fulfilling my obligations to him (read: not keeping my word).

I called a meeting with him and asked what the issue was. He said, "We aligned to go into this market together and you have put a deal in play without me. You didn't keep up your end of the bargain!" I told him that the client knew about the company he used to work with and that they had a bad experience. When I had brought him up, with his history, they had given me explicit instructions not to have him involved in the deal. I also reminded him that I would use him in deals where the fit was good for the client. No fit, no deal.

He told me that I should have fought harder for him to get him in the deal. At that point he pissed me off by telling me how to put deals together, and rather than going head-to-head with him I told him that I was doing what was best for the client and the issue should be closed. I also told him that there would be nothing positive to come out of him continuing to chew my ass so let's agree to consider the issue dealt with and past us.

A week later, I came across a mutual contact who told me that Bill had said I burned him out of a deal. I began to lose my temper, but thought that the conversation may have happened before our meeting. Well, he had said it only the day before, which told me he was still spouting off. I decided to deep-six him. I e-mailed the following to my list of champions:

> Hi all, I wanted to make it explicitly clear that Think Tank and ACME Company are not engaged in a formal relationship nor is there any alliance in place. Both companies are operating in autonomy of one another. Bill Smith is a great financial advisor, but due to circumstances beyond my control, I am no longer able to endorse his services. I do however wish him all the success in the future.
>
> Sincerely,
>
> Chris.

What are my options if I get deep-sixed?

Option 1: Find a new business opportunity. If you have been deep-sixed in your company, you are going to feel the effects of the deep-six reverberate over time. If I had been deep-sixed, I'd look for a new opportunity if I didn't think I could garner power. Women who experience this in a professional firm should start to formulate a Plan B and look to move to a different firm.

Option 2: Garner power. The one sure-fire way to inoculate yourself from a potential deep-six, or to treat a dose of the deep-six, is to accumulate power. You can do this by getting people in your network who are more powerful than the people doing the deep-six.

Now this will be tricky because it might not be clear who deep-sixed you, so you'll need to hunt up major talent for your network. Remember that for men access to people is a powerful tool. The second way to accumulate power is to increase your profitability. The only thing more powerful than reputation is one's ability to generate revenue. There are so few people who are earners in the business world. When you become one, you jump up about 10 levels in people's perception. (If you are an earner, you write your own ticket in business.)

Remember, you are either a driver or a passenger in your professional life. Deciding not to make a decision about taking your career to the next level is a decision and one that is more costly than you know. The deep-six is only effective if you live with the consequences of it rather than taking steps to make the deep-six effects irrelevant.

Gaining Respect: Earning Your Sailing Stripes

What are some of the things that men respect about female colleagues?

- Ability to generate and close deals—This is number one for a reason. At the end of the day, the hunters are honored and welcome at the table. Be an earner.
- Keeps her word on promises — It is really important to men that a person keeps her word. Keeping your word is a strong currency that we put a lot of value in.
- Acts professionally and is reliable under pressure — Everyone can perform when everything is perfect, but the measure of a professional is how she acts when the shit hits the fan. Does she take control of the situation or does she fall apart? If you keep your head about you and are strong and confident during a crisis, you will get major respect from male counterparts.
- Honors and appreciates goal setting and achievement — Because men are goal driven, it is something we respect in other professionals. I personally welcome the opportunity to work with women who take enjoyment in targeting deals and then go after them. This is something I share with all the men I know.
- Being of strong character/not being a pushover — If you are a pile-on, you will get no respect from any of your male counterparts. If you let people treat you without respect, accept poor treatment,

and allow people to dump work on you, we won't respect you. Instead we may look for ways to dump work on you.

- Being open to taking a risk — Women have a reputation for being risk adverse. Many women would call this being responsible. Risk is a necessary part of building business, and if you are adverse to it, you'll be put to the back of the line. The great thing about women focusing on process is you can minimize the risk but still look like you are going out on a limb. One client of mine is totally fearless when it comes to calling any CEO of a company she wants to work with. I respect this immensely about her.

- Being loyal — I think men got this from the military mindset (regardless of whether they've served): "Loyalty above all else. Never leave a man behind." We hold strong our desire to be considered loyal and to have those in our circle loyal to us. The quickest way someone can get deep-sixed by me is to betray my trust. When you speak ill of others, criticize, or share information that you shouldn't, you aren't being loyal and you will be deep-sixed. If you are able to be loyal in all your dealings, you will gain the trust of your colleagues and be held in high regard.

- Honesty — Although honesty is sometimes hard to swallow, anyone with character will respect an individual's ability to be honest, even if it might have a detrimental effect personally.

- Integrity and ethics — In the new paradigm of business that is emerging, all professionals are looking for a higher level of integrity and ethics. Integrity will carry you far in professional circles because people will know you aren't out to screw them over.

- Having a powerful network at her disposal — Remember, you don't need to know everything; you just have to have access to people who know how to do everything. Your network is your most honored and valuable asset in business. If you have a powerful network, it shows your male colleagues that you are a player and are able to access people you need to do the deals you want to do.

These 10 things are all areas that you have complete control over. Take note of this list and focus on developing each of these areas of your professional life. Regardless of your gender, these are important characteristics for all professionals.

Epilogue

This is simply the start of a conversation that is long overdue. I started this book in 2002. My first intention was for it to be a manual that clients would read before working with me. The same questions came up over and over again in sessions, and I thought that by having something for them to read we could move quickly to business development conversations. I remember first telling some male friends I was writing a book for clients and they looked down their noses at me and rolled their eyes. Here's some of what they said, "You sucked in school, what the hell are you going to write?" "All that stuff everyone already knows," "That's all we need, for you to be walking around calling yourself an author," "What's the point, no one will ever publish it?" Keep in mind that these were comments from my friends. It didn't get to me, though. Once I set my mind to something, I do it, especially after I tell people I will. I walked down to *La Mascotte*, a favorite diner in Kitsilano (my neighborhood). I sat down with a notebook and a pen and stared at the cover. What the hell was I going to say? What would people be interested in reading? Then it struck me. This book wasn't about them, me, or anything else. It was about turning on a light and sharing something that hadn't otherwise been seen.

I decided on my inspiration for the book. If I had time to write a book for a woman that I loved, whether it is my wife, mother, sister, or female friend, knowing that she was going to enter the business world and my only advice would be in a book, what would I say? How could I share with her all the things I've witnessed, deconstructed, analyzed, and interpreted over my years in business? What information could make working with Alphas easier and empower her to be authentic, direct, and powerful in business? In this book, I have written all my thoughts in what I believe to be practical applications. I'm not a psychologist, a gender specialist, or a sociologist. I am an Alpha who used to be a total bastard to women, and now I try to live in the position of being women's most passionate advocate. I hope as you read this book you felt that I was speaking directly to you because that was my intent. I want you to know so that you can look at your actions and the actions of your female colleagues and take back your power and authentic self and stop paying the price you think you need to pay for being a woman. You are an equal, but we cannot give it to you, you must claim it.

I want this to be a start of a conversation, not *the* conversation. I don't want you to read this and then have it up on a shelf as a resource. I want this to empower you, to educate you, to inspire you, and at times to piss you off. I want you to know what's going on whether you like it or not. I want you to know that if something comes up you are unsure of you can reference back to this knowing that there are nuggets of information to support you in finding a path that works for you. Once you know, you can't un-know. Once you are familiar with the information, you will be able to implement it daily. Any of you who have read the books out there written by women for women on how to deal with me, I want you to see the real deal here. I'm in the boardroom, I'm in the deal, and I'm in the audience. I've been watching with judgment, and I want you to know what's working and where you are giving up your power to Alpha Males, who not only don't deserve it, but also will use it against you. You will note that this isn't written like a traditional book. It is an extended letter I'm writing to you.

I read a lot of books and go to a lot of lectures, and I have one thing in mind: Where's the nugget? To me the nugget is the piece I can take right now and use. I can make things better for myself for having this nugget of information. I want you to look for the nuggets in this book. Look for yourself and look for nuggets for others. As exceptional communicators, women have a responsibility to share information with those who need it. Have conversations with the women in your life who you work with, with the women you love, and with the men you love. Men (Alphas) will think that you should already know much of this information. They think it is obvious because they have been exposed to it their whole lives. The new paradigm is here, and the plane is on autopilot. Women must take on their authentic leadership roles and lead us in the new model. You and I share this responsibility, and I promise to continue doing my part in spreading the word. Once you have read this book or attend the seminars, the responsibility is then shared by you. An important place to start sharing this information is with your daughters.

Last fall I was keynoting a Junior Achievement event in Vancouver. They do a leadership conference for young women (17 and 18 year olds) and have about 200 women attend. This was my second year doing it, and prior to going on stage I was in the greenroom with a bunch of the speakers and some of the handlers. A mother who had heard my speech the previous year came up to me and said, "I wish you wouldn't do your presentation to these girls." I was a bit shocked and asked her why. She replied, "They are too young. I don't want them to know this stuff yet. Business can be cruel, and I guess I want them protected for a bit longer from the reality." I looked at her and said, "The only thing worse than them knowing is them not knowing and trying to figure out what is going on. Let's give them all the preparation we can to make sure they continue being proud powerful women." As I walked down the hallway to the stage with a bit of a heavy heart I started to question why women would want this stuff not talked about. Then it hit me. . . the mom doesn't think things are going to change. And she is right. If this conversation stops with this book, it will not change. If I pass the torch and it goes out, the darkness will stay. If, however, you continue the conversation around this topic with other women, you will spread the message and bring more and more light to the subject. Many women have worked harder than they had to, but that can and must stop here. It is going to take all of us to get the message out that a powerful woman is the main ingredient to the new paradigm of business.

After talking with that mother at Junior Achievement and realizing that not all women believe things will change, I made the decision right at that point to prove her and other critics wrong. This information is passed through conversations, and we all have a responsibility to share it. I walked up on the stage, looked out at 200 young smiling faces and bright eyes, and said, "Ladies, can I tell you a secret?"

Index